NURTURING NATURE

A Guide to Gardening for Special Needs

Jill Mays

author of *Your Child's Motor Development Story*

NURTURING NATURE:

A Guide to Gardening for Special Needs

All marketing and publishing rights guaranteed to and reserved by:

FUTURE HORIZONS

(817) 277-0727

www.fhautism.com

ISBN: 978-1-963367-05-8

PRAISE FOR *NURTURING NATURE*

"*Nurturing Nature* provides lots of practical, fun gardening activities for children. They will learn that nature is much more interesting than electronic devices."

— Dr. Temple Grandin

"*Nurturing Nature* is a nuanced and practical resource for students, families, and interdisciplinary professionals. This creative and promising approach can be integrated with a range of therapeutic services which aim to educate, empower, and heal across the lifespan."

— Michael J. Schultz, EdD, Senior Fellow Child Welfare League of America, author of *Systems Consultation When Trauma Strikes: Stories of Hope, Collaboration, and Change*

"Jill Mays has written a beautiful, instructive book that speaks to the importance of gardening and celebrating local food while educating about the health of our bodies, community, and environment. An expert in sensory motor and nature-based play, she adeptly outlines the how and the why of gardens—and does so in an inclusive way for those with special needs. A must-read for all those looking to nurture both nature and health!"

— Francie Randolph, EdM, Founding Director, Sustainable CAPE

"This book offers a guide to providing a novel, creative and productive therapeutic approach to motor and sensory interventions in a fun filled environment to persons of any age with special needs. It is likely that the love of gardening will be instilled in many who participate in this program while improving their physical and mental health."

— Dr Bauman, founding director of the Integrated Center for Child Development, LURIE CENTER, The Autism Research Foundation (TARF), The Autism Research Consortium (TARC), and The Autism Treatment Network (ATN)

CONTENTS

CHAPTER ONE

Introduction

G rowing healthy food for my growing family was the rationale I used to enlist my husband's help supervising our children when he got home from work, but in truth, I began gardening to escape the incessant (albeit—joyful) chatter of my three preschoolers. I savored the calm, breathing in the fresh smell of the soil and the aerosols of evergreens wafting in the breeze as the sun sank behind the western hills. Due to towering oaks surrounding our property, our harvest diminished as the trees leafed out, shading my garden. Frustrated with limited sunlight and predatory four-legged foragers, we eventually shifted our gardening aspirations to our cottage in Truro, at the tip of Cape Cod.

Each summer I'd check out armloads of garden books (this was the pre-internet era) from the Truro Library. Maggie Hanelt, the Director

of Youth Services noticed. Having published a book about sensory motor development for children, she recognized my aligned interests of gardening and kids, so she introduced me to Francie Randolph, one of the founders of Sustainable CAPE (Center for Agricultural Preservation and Education) and the Truro Community Children's Garden, located behind the library. I became involved with the weekly group, and expanded my volunteer time to help Stephanie Rein, a gifted educator and farmer, in the Farmer in the School program she created. As an occupational therapist, I had expertise in working with special needs populations, so when Maggie asked if I'd run a garden group for disabled adults, I gladly accepted.

This book is a culmination of my experiences working side-by-side with market farmers, who generously shared tricks of the trade. Through my observations of children, from the smallest toddler to adolescents with boundless energy, and coaching small groups of adults, I have come to appreciate the enormous impact gardening can have. The lessons I have learned over the years seem too important to keep to myself. So, I share them with you.

Normally, Max can't stand still, but after working in the garden for the past hour he waits patiently to fill his goodie bag with vegetables. Thanks to the collective effort of the community ten years ago, Truro, a rural town with a little over two thousand full-time residents, built a small garden with raised beds enclosed by a fence. It sits behind the

Chapter One

Truro Library, which provided the land. Unlike other community gardens, this one caters to children. Now, a pile of compost sits by the shed. Max spent most of his time shoveling compost into buckets and hauling it to garden beds for side-dressing the plants, providing added nourishment to ensure a bountiful harvest. All the heavy lifting activated nerves in his muscles and joints that charged up filters in his brain. So now he's calm and happy as he lets the younger children grab fistfuls of veggies first.

Olivia's bag overflows with nasturtium. Throughout the group time, she pleads for us to let her eat the peppery-tasting blossoms growing in the garden. While few adults eat flowers, the farmer has added edible flowers and herbs that provide beauty, sweet and pungent aromas, and interesting textures, along with attracting butterflies and other beneficial insects. As Olivia has discovered, more than a garnish, the flowers taste delicious!

Charlie lines up eager to stuff his bag with green beans he's tasted for the first time. A fussy eater, he never touches vegetables, but after planting seeds and watching them grow all season, he powered up and tried a crisp green pod. To his astonishment, he liked it! Over the ten years of the garden's existence, the overriding premise has been validated repeatedly: when children grow food, they learn to love eating it. Perhaps it's the pride of creating actual food, or the taste difference of fresh organic produce. Compared to the tasteless items traveling thousands of miles in container ships before making it to the grocery store, the fruits and vegetables pulled out of the ground have a delectable flavor. Time and again, children learn to eat food they have never tried before!

A garden volunteer beckons Tyler to come join the group for the harvest feast. He has lingered in the garden to play with a squiggly worm. After learning the importance of worms in creating rich, fertile soil, Tyler has become an ardent champion. Once terrified to touch the wriggling crawlers, he now rescues the worms exposed when the soil gets dug up. After thanking the worm for its contribution to the garden, Tyler runs over to the picnic table to join the others.

Cucumbers and beans are piled on a platter, festooned with the orange and yellow nasturtium for all to eat. After sampling the lemon cucumbers and comparing the taste of red versus yellow cherry tomatoes, children clasp goody bags filled with vegetables to share with their families when they go home.

The Truro Community Children's Garden welcomes children of all ages. The program expands and contracts with the seasons. As a small rural community, a handful of local kids brave the icy Atlantic winds of early spring to prep raised beds and plant seeds. By July, vacationers have arrived and the group sometimes swells to over twenty. Coming from all over the globe, children represent a wide variety of backgrounds. Many have special needs. All are welcome at the garden.

Why Garden?

Growing healthy, fresh food and creating attractive outdoor spaces are obvious benefits of gardening. Getting outside and disconnecting from electronic devices is another. But the inherent value goes much deeper, touching many aspects of our lives.

Chapter One

Truro Children's Garden

While a garden plot has no resemblance to a gym, the physicality required to garden strengthens core muscles, legs, and arms. Navigating around plants and raised beds requires balance. Weeding and seeding develop fine motor skills and hand-eye coordination. Gardening often requires the use of two hands, tapping into bilateral motor coordination as well.

Max doesn't feel like he's having a therapy session, but doing all that heavy lifting activates the same neurological systems that the school therapist tweaks by having him play on large balls and scooters. Tyler and Charlie both struggle with hypersensitivities to touch, but outside in the garden, the mixture of sensations and physical work helps mitigate their discomfort. They become more resilient and courageous in touch exploration.

A sensory seeker, Olivia gets plenty as she roams around the swirl of colors and fragrances, snitching flowers to fire up her taste buds. Sensations flourish in a garden. For some, working the soil is a soothing experience. Like Tyler and Charlie, those who struggle with touch sensations have the opportunity to become more flexible in their tactile engagement. When provided with the proper equipment, they can overcome many touch sensitivities.

Benefits of Gardening for Children

A child can work on puzzles and a variety of computer games to improve visual perception, but in the garden, visual challenges abound. Visual discrimination is required to identify weeds from tender seedlings. Planting tiny seeds demands focus and attention. The varied colors and shapes of the vegetation pull on our attention. Butterflies flitting around augment the pleasurable visual experience.

Gardening provides a myriad of learning opportunities. Measuring and counting are taught in math class, but a lot more fun to do outside. Seed and plant labels require writing. Even the youngest child can understand simple science concepts. Plants need food, water, space, and sunlight, just like people.

Many individuals struggle with social engagement. When working in the garden, interaction can occur on many levels. At the most basic level, parallel interaction can occur, such as quietly weeding side by side.

Chapter One

Other jobs require cooperation, helping to build more advanced social skills and team building. A sense of community develops with shared tasks, goals, and bountiful outcomes.

Beyond the potential skill development, research has shown that being outside in natural settings reduces stress and improves physical and emotional health. Gardening is a journey. It's a creative process, a sustaining practice, and empowering to all who partake. And at the end of the road, there's magic: tiny seeds transform into nourishing food and flowers, and a patch of dirt is converted into a sensory wonderland filled with enticing aromas, textures, sounds, and visual beauty.

Children love to eat the food that they grow!

Benefits of Gardening for Adults with Special Needs

As the Children's Garden grew, many in the broader community took an interest. Cape Abilities, an adult program that provides therapeutic and social supports for individuals with disabilities throughout Cape Cod, became aware of Truro's garden. They volunteered to make a wheelchair-accessible raised garden bed and donated plants from the Cape Abilities farm. With my background as an occupational therapist, I took the lead in running a weekly garden group. The group meets weekly from April until it's too cold to work outside, usually early November. Adult participants range in age from twenty-two to seventy plus.

We begin with a weekly garden tour. Traversing a rambling path through an edible landscape, the group checks out the blueberry bushes and raspberry canes to see if any berries remain. Fred, a taciturn middle-aged man in the program, demonstrates his horticulture acumen by identifying many of the plants we observe.

After the stroll, we get to work pulling up mint that has run amok and needs thinning. Jane grew up surrounded by gardeners. At seventy years old, she still loves to squat down and pull up weeds. With eyesight waning, her ability to discriminate weeds from tender seedlings is not strong, so before she begins yanking, the area to weed is clearly marked off for her.

Emmy prefers to sit alone and avoids talking to others. In years past, she was reluctant to join in the group activities. But she loves to pot up seedlings and bring them home to plant in her family garden, so little by little, she became a more active participant. Now Emmy not only joins in willingly, but helps others with small tasks when requested, elevating her social interactions to the cooperative level.

Sandy, an energetic young woman, is knowledgeable, is proficient in tasks requiring manual dexterity, and loves helping others. But she hates to get her hands dirty. Once reassured that she had ample opportunity to wipe off her hands and wash them thoroughly when done with a gardening chore, she dug in.

When George arrived in a wheelchair, he had no difficulty working on the Cape Abilities herb box. His chair tucked underneath the thirty-inch high raised bed comfortably. He had easy access to weed, water, and transplant parsley and basil.

During our sessions, the group pots up individual plants to take with them. This week, the mint they just pulled up gets transplanted into small containers. As the group boards the van, they clutch pots of mint, which they'll take home to their own gardens.

The trip takes an hour from the Cape Abilities center, but staff and participants agree it's worth the long drive. They love the sensory smorgasbord: vibrant colors, the savory aroma of culinary herbs, bird song, and on windy days, a low rumble of the surf nearby. Along with the rich smells, soothing sounds, and naturescape that facilitates well-being, they learn simple facts and concepts about gardening and nature. The group works as a team. It is a happy time—a weekly celebration.

This book is titled *A Guide to Gardening for Special Needs*. We all have special needs. I had a need to escape from my kids for a few precious moments a week. Over time, this need morphed into the desire to

*The Cape Abilities Garden participants enjoy walking
through the Truro Library's "Edible Landscape" each week.*

create a bountiful and visually appealing garden. Children have a need to immerse themselves in natural environments and the opportunity to move around. Adults have the need to disconnect from the digital world and de-stress. The elderly have a need to remain physically active and socially connected to stay healthy and independent.

Chapter One

Vulnerable populations, such as the neurodiverse and physically challenged, are at great risk of suffering from isolation and stress-related illnesses. Finding ways to maintain physical fitness and social engagement is key to enhancing the quality of their lives.

Gardening has been proven to be especially beneficial to physical, cognitive, and emotional health. For the uninitiated, gardening may seem like a daunting or insurmountable project. This guide shows how the uninitiated can begin gardening: from the smallest pot of flowers to a large, flourishing plot of land. The guide outlines why gardening is critical to everyone's health and provides step-by-step instructions on how to go about creating a garden. Specific activities, ways to adapt tasks to accommodate special needs, and benefits gained from the activities are reviewed. Special considerations for specific populations are highlighted. Finally, recent findings on the health benefits of gardening are reviewed. By the time you read this entire guide, you will be armed with all the information and resources you need to get started:

- *Chapter 2* highlights the many health and developmental benefits: Simply stepping outside offers many healthful dividends. Working in a garden augments and develops critical skills for health and well-being.

- *Chapter 3* reviews all the sensory systems and the positive impact of nature: Our senses help us engage in the world and have a strong influence on our emotions. Nature can tweak our emotions in powerful and beneficial ways.

- *Chapter 4* reviews everything you need to know to get started in creating a garden: This chapter covers all the basics for starting a

garden, from essential equipment to the best way to plant and grow a bountiful harvest.

- *Chapter 5* lists recommended activities to do throughout the year: Activities are provided from the darkest, coldest months in the winter, through spring, summer, and the final months of the year.
- *Chapter 6* offers guidelines, equipment recommendations, and best practices for individuals with physical and visual impairments.
- *Chapter 7* delves deeper into the scientific evidence of how nature and gardening impacts everyone and offers amazing health benefits. Special attention to studies supporting the positive impact of gardening on special populations is provided, focusing especially on the neurodiverse and aging populations.

CHAPTER
TWO

Health and Physical Benefits of Gardening

I n the adult garden group I run, some of the participants are eager beavers, burrowing their hands in the soil, totally immersing themselves in all aspects of the garden experience. Others stroll around, observing the garden flora, but aren't so keen on chores like weeding. Squatting down might be too physically demanding. For those who have tactile hypersensitivities, touching the soil feels repugnant. Working in close proximity to others may feel uncomfortable. A casual observer of our group might question what benefits are derived from such passive participation. This chapter reviews the many benefits of gardening. From the reluctant participant to the ardent nature lover and stalwart workhorse, all report feeling happier and calmer when they leave.

Sunny Days

Simply standing outside absorbing the sun's rays has many benefits. Even on a cloudy spring day, indoor light can't match the sun's strength. Sunshine gives us vitamin D, with many proven benefits for short and long-term health. Vitamin D is produced when ultraviolet rays (UV rays) from sunlight strike the skin and trigger vitamin D synthesis. Vitamin D promotes calcium and phosphorus absorption to maintain healthy bones and prevent cramping of muscles. It's needed for bone growth. Without enough vitamin D, bones become brittle. Vitamin D protects older adults from osteoporosis, decreases inflammation, and increases immune function.

Experts recommend five to thirty minutes of exposure between 10:00 AM and 4:00 PM daily, without sunscreen, which blocks the UV rays. (The minimum exposure is recommended for those who burn easily.) Along with bone and muscle health, vitamin D has been found to lower the risk of types 1 and 2 diabetes: autoimmune diseases such as rheumatoid arthritis, psoriasis, and polymyalgia rheumatica; and

FUN FACT

In the winter in northern latitudes (40th parallel and above) the UV rays are not strong enough to produce vitamin D. For example:

- Boston, Massachusetts – 4 months
- Edmonton, Canada – 5 months
- Bergen, Norway – 6 months

You need to supplement during those dark days!

thyroid diseases. In one large-scale study, lower levels of vitamin D led to a 54 percent higher risk of dementia. Other studies have identified an increased risk of developing multiple sclerosis and suffering from upper respiratory diseases when vitamin D levels are depressed.

In addition to the production of vitamin D, recent studies have revealed that exposure to sunlight stimulates a process in the retina that controls the shape of the developing eye. Decreased time outside and the absence of sunlight lead to myopia, or nearsightedness. So sunshine helps us see the world better—literally!

The Magic of Trees

Walking, or even just standing near trees, can have a beneficial effect. Trees emit aerosols that calm, soothe, and even help us stay healthy. The fragrant smell of pine and other trees comes from chemicals that actually activate disease-killing cells in the body, boosting the immune system and our ability to fight off infections and stay healthy. That feel-good experience we have when we smell fresh pine actually does make us feel better ... and scientific studies have explained how. The last chapter will review many of these studies to help you understand the powerful impact of trees on our health and well-being.

Other studies demonstrate that spending time in the natural world can reduce anxiety. Simply looking at trees, plants, open spaces, and the sky have many beneficial effects on the brain. Along with a calming effect, these naturescapes foster a sense of well-being, creativity, and focus.

NURTURING NATURE

Walking on a garden tour may not seem like an Olympic sport, but for many tethered to electronic devices, or simply living in homebound situations, the walks increase cardio-vascular fitness, activate muscles, and stimulate joints. While not especially rigorous, these health benefits sure beat out energy expended by the proverbial "couch potato."

Most of the participants in my group choose to participate in the actual work: weeding, planting, and harvesting. Core muscles get strengthened when bending and stooping down to engage in these activities. Using a trowel increases the strength of the forearm, wrist, and hand muscles. Shoveling is a major workout for both large and small muscles. Anyone who's shoveled snow can appreciate the cardio-vascular benefit of scooping up compost from a pile to dump on the garden bed.

While physically engaged in garden tasks, subtle but significant changes occur. Weight-bearing happens when walking, carrying, and pushing heavy things around. These activities stimulate the joints, which strengthens the bones. This is especially important for the elderly population, who frequently suffer from osteoporosis and the worry of fractures. Weight-bearing also facilitates healthy bone growth in children and adolescents.

Finally, these activities build physical endurance. With all of the participants in my garden group, I find that over time, each member engages more. Some need to rest and skip a portion of our walking tour when they first join the group. Within a few weeks, they remain with the group for the entire walk. For the reluctant gardener, I initially suggest they complete a small, well-defined amount of work. For example: pull up five weeds. The next week, up the ante to ten, and so on. By the end of the season, the group clears out most of a garden bed with minimal coaxing and direction.

We'll get into the weeds (aka: details) of the many ways gardening augments physical skills. For children, gardening helps develop critical skills for motor coordination. For the adult population, the physicality of gardening helps maintain or improve motor competence. In the elderly, moving is critical for maintaining the integrity of joints and mobility. Studies on Alzheimer's and dementia underscore the imperative of keeping physically active as the best way to limit brain deterioration.

Facilitating Bilateral Motor Coordination

Many garden tasks require the use of two hands: raking, shoveling, and transplanting, to name a few. Even the simple task of plucking beans from the vine works better using two hands: one hand pulls a bean off while the other hand stabilizes the vine, preventing the plant from getting torn from the ground.

While using two hands, a message is sent to both sides of the brain. When bilateral movement occurs, there are places in the nervous system where crossover or communication of the motor signal occurs. Crossovers begin in the spinal cord and continue in the brain, where there is interhemispheric communication. Essentially, information travels from one side of the brain to the other. With bilateral movements, the brain receives signals from both sides of the body and transfers the information to the opposite side of the brain. In essence, the right side of the brain talks to the left side and vice-versa.

Why is this important? Learning occurs best when there is fluid communication or pathways established in the brain. The bilateral input is like a neurological workout. The more you bombard the system with stimuli, the more efficient and organized the pathways become. Just as you need repetition in an exercise workout to strengthen muscles, the brain needs input to build pathways. Doing two-handed tasks required for gardening helps lay down these pathways, building superhighways for a more fluid flow of information in the brain, making it easier to learn, adapt, and engage with the world.

Most two-handed activities require reaching. For instance, when raking, the left hand guides the rake, while the right arm reaches across the body to assist in pulling. As the arm reaches, core muscles are activated. Muscles that wrap around from the front to the back get strengthened, improving flexibility, the ability to maintain upright positions, and balance. This is especially important for the elderly. With fewer opportunities to engage in activities that require reaching, core muscle strength decreases and balance issues surface.

For children, reaching across the body is important for a different reason. When young children avoid reaching across the midline, they tend to manipulate things with the hand closest to the object. For instance, a toy on the left side is manipulated with the left hand, even if the child is right-handed. When this occurs, a preferred dominance is slow to develop. With gardening tasks, reaching across the midline of the body occurs spontaneously. Core muscles grow stronger, and more spontaneous movements occur, leading to the establishment of hand preference.

Hand-Eye Motor Coordination

Hand-eye motor coordination begins moments after birth. As an infant's eyes open and focus on the caretaker, this developmental process begins. Getting babies' sustained visual attention is key, so we jangle keys and colorful rattles in their visual field, moving them slowly so the eyes follow. Eventually, babies begin swatting at toys and the hand-eye connection begins.

When we think of hand-eye coordination, things like catching a ball and playing tennis come to mind. But almost everything we do requires the pairing of visual attention to guide the hands. This guidance leads to flexibility and efficacy in performing tasks. Opportunities for building competence in this area are important. The key is to tweak visual attention with bright colors, varied shapes, and patterns. Adding novel textures, visual attention is drawn to the hand to figure out what caused the unusual touch sensation. Add olfactory stimuli, and individuals might scan the immediate area to identify the source of the smell, like a sprig of mint, for instance. Holding the herb to smell solidifies the connection.

Gardens offer a smorgasbord of colors, shapes, textures and smells. The eyes are bombarded, and the visual system comes alive. Pungent smells intermingle with herbaceous and sweet aromas, which can draw visual attention to discover the source of the smell. Every gardening task

*Beautiful flower gardens can pique our visual
attention and make us feel happy!*

requires visual attention to guide hand movements. Weeding requires
the identification of unwanted plants. When transferring compost from
the wheelbarrow to the garden bed, the eyes need to guide the shovel.
Placing tiny seeds one inch apart in a garden bed requires intense focus.

Just as a baby progresses from batting a mobile, to a slow rolling ball,
to bopping a balloon, gardening affords a gradation of visual attention
and hand coordination. These varied demands allow for success at all
functional levels. Shoveling and piling mulch on beds requires minimal
focus on details. Likewise with watering: hold a watering can over a
plant, and tip the spout. Voilà—success in watering the thirsty plant!
But eyes still have to see the watering can and the plant to water.

Weeding can be a simple visual task—identify a circumscribed area
full of unwanted vegetation and yank it up. But the hand still has to
grasp each plant, and the eyes guide the hand to do this. Want a bigger

challenge? Discriminate between clover (weed) and an emerging parsley seedling, which look similar. This requires meticulous observation while the fingers pinch and gently pull up the clover, careful not to disturb the shallow roots of the parsley seedling.

Planting can be as simple as tossing seeds on top of the soil (broadcasting). The level of challenge and complexity, like using a fine pincer grasp to place tiny seeds in carefully measured-out spacing in rows, helps refine skills not only in hand-eye coordination but also fine motor dexterity.

Recognizing weeds from tender seedlings requires visual focus.

Fine Motor Coordination

Having children work in the garden bolsters the development of fine motor skills. For adults, honing garden skills helps maintain and even improve dexterity. For the elderly, "use it or lose it" applies. Without regular movement, hands weaken and joints become compromised. Pain and difficulty performing daily life tasks ensue.

As mentioned earlier in the chapter, gardening strengthens muscles, and this includes the small muscles in the hands. Holding a trowel or even clutching a watering can strengthens the muscles for grasping. Stronger muscles provide better support for aging joints. Elderly individuals struggling with arthritis and related conditions will benefit from gentle tasks that keep muscles strong. Moving the hands also aids with blood flow and moving fluid in swollen hands.

A refined pinch is critical to get through the day without frustrating blunders. Using a key and eating with utensils require finger dexterity. Untwisting the toothpaste cap for brushing teeth requires a sturdy fingertip grasp. A refined pincer grasp is required to pick up and place seeds in a pot or garden bed. Planting seeds helps develop and maintain functioning well beyond the garden.

To keep hands moving throughout the year, bring a few plants inside. Using a plant sprayer to water the plants activates deep hand muscles. These muscles are important for sophisticated fine motor dexterity. Spraying keeps the older hand spry, flexible, and strong. For younger kids, plant sprayers actually help develop the intrinsic muscles for the first time, leading to more refined dexterity.

Lifting, digging, planting, spraying, essentially all the tasks required for gardening, are terrific ways to develop excellent fine motor control and maintain it for a lifetime!

Chapter Two

Motor Planning

Sometimes less is more, and in the case of motor planning, this applies. Motor planning has three basic components. The first relates to the ideation, or know-how of approaching a task. The second relates to the ability to link movements in the proper sequence and execute specific movements simultaneously. The third relates to the quality of execution. It's complicated.

Professional athletes have superior motor planning. Even with the same training as others on a team, they rise above with inherent natural ability. Many in neurodiverse populations struggle with motor planning challenges. Engaging in complex games that demand quick responses and are unpredictable can be stressful. Activities requiring motor planning can increase anxiety, and avoidance leads to isolation.

The great news about gardening is that there are many tasks that require minimal motor planning. Most tasks require familiar movements that are repetitive. Carrying a watering can and tipping it to pour water on each plant requires minimal accuracy. It is a favorite activity from the youngest toddler at the Children's Garden to the oldest members of the Cape Abilities group. Chores like weeding are predictable. Members work side by side doing the same task. Except for the occasional earthworm squiggling by, the garden sits placidly, patiently waiting for attention.

For people who struggle on a daily basis with unknowns and challenges, gardening is a welcome break. It's an opportunity to do a job stress-free and feel a sense of accomplishment when completed.

CHAPTER THREE

Sensory Benefits of Gardening

So far we have focused on *actions*, or motor output that occurs when gardening. But that's only half the story. As we stroll around a garden or settle down in one spot to pull up weeds, our sensory systems are immersed in a myriad of sensations.

When the Truro Children's garden group gathers, they learn how to identify plants by looking at shapes, colors, and sizes. They work the soil, usually with ungloved hands. The group always ends with tasting the food harvested that day.

The Cape Abilities group notes the changes in size and color of plants and fruits growing, and especially enjoys seeing butterflies flitting around. Each week, they receive a sprig of lemon balm and mint to smell. Some get right to work digging, enjoying the feel of working in the soil. Others experience discomfort touching the varied sensations of vegetation and dirt. They need to wash their hands immediately after getting their hands dirty.

Everyone is familiar with the five senses: visual (seeing), auditory (hearing), olfactory (smelling), gustatory (taste), and tactile (touch). Several other senses occur mostly on an unconscious level, but have significant impact on our sense of well-being. These are proprioception (body awareness), kinesthesia (movement), and vestibular (balance and more). Each sense will be reviewed to gain an understanding of how specific sensory input affects us and how nature and gardening can augment the positive aspects of each system. Special attention will be given to issues that frequently occur for neurodiverse individuals and how nature helps mitigate and remediate difficulties.

Touch (The Tactile System)

Humans' first experience with the world comes through the tactile system. After floating around (in utero) for about nine months in a temperature-controlled environment, infants get squeezed through the birth canal and plop out. Often, it takes a smack to get babies breathing and engaged with their new home: planet earth.

Touch is our first link with the world and remains a critical aspect for survival, learning, and pleasure throughout our lives. Touch receptors are located in the skin, which provides a protective barrier to keep us alive. These tactile nerves warn us if something is hot, cold, or painful. The tactile system also helps us explore and learn about our immediate environment. Touch sensations can grab our attention, pique our

Chapter Three

You can find many intriguing textures in nature.
Moss feels like a thick pile of velvety carpet.

interest in learning, soothe us, and help us interact on a physical level to develop deep emotional ties. So it makes sense that with so much work to do, the tactile system has two distinct functions: survival/protection and discrimination/exploration.

The protective aspect of touch links to basic physiological functions (for example: heart and respiration rates) for survival. This harks back to our evolutionary roots. When humans lived in the jungle, feeling an unknown stimuli likely meant a predator was beginning an attack, so the body immediately went into a fight, flight, or freeze response. Over time, we've evolved to override this high-anxiety reaction.

However, some people remain locked in fright, flight, and fight responses. Their protective system still dominates, and they remain hypersensitive to touch. Subsequently, they avoid tactile exploration and often require consistent and predictable environments, surrounding themselves with familiar and (tolerated) things. Here are some examples:

- Fussy about the type of clothing tolerated
- Avoid physical contact with others (even if touch is supportive/loving)
- Limited diet: don't tolerate certain textured foods, which can elicit a gag reflex and vomiting

People who live in this persistent state of disequilibrium suffer from anxiety. Stress-related illnesses may develop. In the effort to cope, tactile defensive individuals may become rigid in daily habits and tend to isolate themselves from others. And by restricting their tactile exploration, they miss out on the pleasures normally derived from touch.

Conscious or not, we all manipulate our tactile systems. When the world locked down for the pandemic and many worked from home, people readily eschewed work outfits for joggers and other comfy clothes. We were all thrust into survival mode, so it made sense that we gravitated to soothing textures.

Along with evoking comfort and pleasure responses, tactile stimuli are highly alerting to the nervous system. So on those days when everyone feels low, with zero energy, dip into a highly loaded tactile experience (like baking bread!), and you'll get energized.

The tactile system has become an integral part of people's ability to navigate the world. Exploration through touch helps build fine motor

Chapter Three

dexterity. Think of how clumsy you are when your fingers become numb. Even visual and spatial reasoning have been linked to touch discrimination. When babies feel a round ball, they learn the concept of circle. When they touch (or bang into) a sharp corner of a table, they discover right angles, long before learning about ninety-degree angles in math class.

Beyond the utilitarian imperatives, tactile input can bring comfort, joy, and even ecstasy. For instance, many people pay a premium for soft textured fabrics like velvet, satin, and cashmere because they bring them comfort. Touch, in the form of stroking, is a commonly used method to soothe infants and children. It is also a powerful component in developing intimacy.

So where does gardening fit into this picture? To gain all the benefits of touch, like exploring the world and developing intimate relationships, the protective system needs to calm down. Gardening provides many opportunities to touch and explore. For individuals who experience tactile hypersensitivities, offering strategies to help cope with their discomfort assists in developing tolerance for their perceived noxious sensations.

In our Cape Abilities group, we employ several methods to help tactile-sensitive individuals get involved with the garden tasks. Working with gloves is an obvious strategy. Knowing that a sink, soap, and towel are available immediately after getting hands dirty helps to cope with the discomfort for short periods. This leads to better tolerance. Eventually, reluctant participants do not hold back, literally digging right into the messy chores.

NURTURING NATURE

Plants for Tactile Pleasure

Flowers and leafed plants:

FERNS: feathery sensation when brushed

LAMB'S EAR: leaves feel very soft

GIANT SILVER MULLEIN: flannel-like (at one time used to line shoes for comfort)

PUSSY WILLOW: soft like fur

CATNIP: light tickly feeling when stroked

BLEEDING HEART: flowers feel tickly, leaves are fern-like and feathery

AMARANTHUS: velvet flowers

For Bare Feet:

MOSS: velvety texture

CREEPING THYMES: scratchy

CLOVER: tickly

Herb/Vegetables:

DILL AND FENNEL: feathery foliage

SAGE: fuzzy leaves

KALE: curly/crinkly

ARTICHOKE: unusual shape, hard knobby leaves

RAINBOW CHARD: waxy smooth and bumpy leaves

SQUASHES: varied textures from smooth to bumpy

Beyond the Garden:

TREE BARKS: varied textures from smooth to scratchy

Vegetation offers varied textures that are inviting to explore. Over time, hypersensitive individuals might be curious and will reach out and touch unusual textures. Kids who struggle with tactile defensiveness often become champions of the squiggly earthworms, getting over their squeamishness to save the crawlers from the shovel when digging occurs. These experiences lead to growing tolerance and flexibility. As the ability to tolerate tactile input improves, the sympathetic nervous system's stress response diminishes. The individual becomes calmer and healthier!

Proprioception (Body Awareness) and Kinesthesia (Movement)

Gardening requires physical labor: digging, shoveling, pulling, and stooping down. Muscles and joints get a good workout. After spending time shoveling compost into a garden bed, you become acutely aware of your joints (sore shoulders, knees ...) and fatigued muscles. While your body might be complaining, your brain feels happy.

Proprioception nerves are found in the joints (shoulders, knees, ankles, etc.) and send messages to inhibitory neurons in the brain. The job of inhibitory neurons is to cancel or get rid of unnecessary sensory stimuli. They are primary filters in the brain.

The nerve fibers in our muscles have a complementary effect. When muscles stretch and contract these kinesthetic nerves activate alerting areas of the brain. The joints and muscles work together, providing a balance of alerting and energizing along with filtering out unnecessary input.

As we move, alerting areas of the brain and filters are activated. Think of the 7th inning stretch at a baseball game, or intermission at a theater production. Sitting still for a long time makes us stiff and groggy. Getting up and moving around helps us focus again.

To help understand the role of filters in the brain, imagine the following two scenarios:

1. You work in an office building on the tenth floor in NY City. There is construction going on nearby. You hear a crash and feel a rumble frequently throughout the day. Soon, you tune out the vibration and noise.

2. You work on the tenth floor in San Bernardino (near the San Andreas Fault). When you feel a vibration and hear a rumble, your heart rate increases and you go into action mode. The body response occurs before you even consider that it might be an earthquake. You dash to the designated safe area.

The California scenario is an appropriate response since the possibility of danger exists. In the New York situation, with well-functioning filters in the brain, you don't shift to a panicked state all day long. If someone gets alarmed every time they hear a crash, they become chronically anxious.

When an individual struggles with environmental sensations (touch, sounds, visual stimuli), they remain in a stress mode. The sympathetic nervous system takes over, leading to physiological stress markers like elevated cortisol levels and high blood pressure. This is why activating filters in the brain is key. With an efficient filtering system, the individual isn't locked into that unhealthy high-alert stress mode.

Chapter Three

The best way to build a more efficient filtering system is to bombard the inhibitory neurons in the brain with lots of input from the joints. Every activity that requires movement activates this complex system: kinesthetic (movement) stimulation for alerting, balanced with proprioceptive (body awareness) stimuli, which activates filters, so the body can make a measured, appropriate response.

Gardening offers a large dose of heavy work, the prime instigator of activating the filtering system. An individual might hate getting their hands dirty while working, but the heavy work of yanking up weeds

☀ FUN FACT

The brain is made up of approximately 86 billion nerve cells that communicate in up to 1,000 trillion connections! Each second the human body sends 11 million bits per second to the brain for processing:

- Eyes – 10,000,000 per second
- Skin – 1,000,000 per second
- Ears – 100,000 per second
- Taste – 1,000 per second

The conscious mind can only process 50 bits per second, so there's a lot of compression and filtering that takes place. That's why having a robust filtering system (and proprioception) is so important!

while stooping down or digging with a trowel activates proprioceptors, thereby mitigating the perceived noxious touch sensation. The end result is the ability to tolerate tactile stimuli better!

I look for heavy work activities for all the populations I work with because there are so many benefits. With a robust filtering system, individuals experience the following:

- A feeling of calm
- Improved focus and attention
- Decreased distractibility
- Reduced anxiety
- Increased feelings of well-being and happiness

 Heavy Work Activities

- Carrying watering can
- Carrying baskets of harvested vegetables
- Digging
- Shoveling

- Raking
- Pushing a wheelbarrow
- Stooping over to plant/weed
- Kneeling to plant/weed

 ## Auditory (Hearing)

For centuries we have used sound to evoke emotions. Think of an orchestral symphony. Quick beats and high notes convey happiness, while the melancholy chords of a cello evoke sadness and longing. Add the pounding of kettledrums, and you sense danger. Often your heart

Chapter Three

speeds up or slows down in response to the sound. The motion picture industry has used soundtracks effectively to heighten suspense. (Who can forget the simple alternating pattern of the two notes E and F in the movie *Jaws*?)

Many of us use music to regulate our mood and energy levels. Wake up in the morning and need a jolt to get going? Maybe R & B will do the trick. Tough day at work? Some listen to classical music to calm down. Others need heavy metal or rap to stamp out negative feelings.

Hearing occurs when sound waves, made up of vibrating molecules, enter the ear, channeling into the canal where sound amplifies. The waves hit an oval membrane, which vibrates. Tiny bones pick up from there, amplifying the sound. Finally, deep in the inner ear, twenty-five thousand nerve endings respond to the vibrations by transforming them into electrical impulses. These get sent to the brain via the auditory nerve. Phew!

Scientists have been studying the effects of sound on our emotions and health for decades. Recent studies have noted the adverse effects urban and mechanical sounds have on our health. Other studies highlight the beneficial effects sounds of nature have on our well-being.

Noise-canceling devices help people concentrate and sleep. Sounds at various frequencies calm the brain, helping to ameliorate conditions such as anxiety and depression. Low frequencies such as bass and sacred drumming ground people. Georgian chants offer neutral, soothing background music, while the higher pitches (high frequencies) lead to more esoteric responses. Tibetan flutes, bells, and bowls evoke meditation and spiritual healing.

Not surprising, sounds in nature run the gamut of frequencies, from the low rumble of thunder to the high-pitched trill of a robin. The sound of wind varies depending on its ferocity, from a gentle breeze to fierce low- or high-pitched howling. One of the first signs of spring is the return of bird song. Sit near a cluster of flowers, and the buzz of honeybees will draw your attention. A pot of deep pink and red blossoms will entice hummingbirds, whose whirring wings create a low vibration. Spring heralds a chorus of tiny wood frogs or peepers with their high-pitched chirping sounds. As summer rolls in, the sound of crickets, katydids, and grasshoppers fill the air, especially in the night when the world settles into quietude. If you live near a pond or lake, the croak of bullfrogs might lull you to sleep. Water sounds, such as a babbling brook, the rhythm of waves, and the pounding of waterfalls, have a soothing effect. Even as the days shorten and much of the verdant

FUN FACT

Bird Song song has been found to increase attention and mood!

In one study, 1,300 participants assessed their well-being three times a day, related to the environment they were in. The researchers found a significant positive association between seeing or hearing birds and improved mental well-being, which persisted over time. If participants saw or heard a bird, their mental health remained higher hours later.

Another study found that after healthy participants listened to six-minute audio clips of bird song, they experienced reduced feelings of depression, anxiety, and paranoia.

Chapter Three

world turns brown, the rustling of falling leaves and the crunch of dried leaf litter in autumn has a pleasant sensation, perhaps evoking memories of running through piles of leaves during childhood.

Many studies have documented the detrimental effect of urban sounds, such as vehicular traffic, airplanes, and construction. Lower academic performance in school children, increased health maladies, higher anxiety, and related emotional conditions correlate with noisy environments. Yet, most humans live in urban areas, so what can be done?

Nature protects us from the vagaries of noise pollution. Trees and bushes sequester and absorb the noise, so it becomes muffled. Just walking a couple dozen yards away from a busy avenue, tucked behind some vegetation decreases stress levels. Bird song and the sound of gurgling water have been shown to mitigate the noxious sounds of urban life, even if it doesn't cancel it out. Subjects in one study still heard the city noise, but their attention was drawn to the pleasant sound of flowing water. For those who cannot escape to a tree-lined park, incorporating nature sounds into playlists for work, school, and living spaces mollifies the negative consequences of noise pollution.

NURTURING NATURE

For individuals who struggle with auditory hypersensitivity every day, the soothing sounds of nature can have a mitigating effect. Whether relying on noise-canceling devices to help block out intrusive noise, or actually going outside, the sounds of nature draw attention away from the obtrusive to the fascinating, like the buzz of a bee or the trill of a cardinal. Interest sparks pleasure areas of the brain, which, of course, makes us happy.

Plants for Listening Pleasure

NON-INVASIVE BAMBOO: like a subtle wind chime and rustling leaves

FIG TREE: rustling leaves

WEEPING BIRCH AND WILLOW: branches make a swishing sound of branches in breeze

HONESTY: rattling sound of papery seed casings

GRASSES: swishing sound

EUPHORBIA LATHYRISM: clicking sound of seeds

SUNFLOWERS: buzzing sound from the many bees they attract

RED AND DEEP PINK FLOWERS: whirring wings of the hummingbirds they attract

Any dense foliage will sequester noise pollution.
Pines provide foliage year round.

Chapter Three

 Olfactory (Smelling)

While sounds can alter our immediate mood, scents have a strong link to emotions and memories. Smell occurs when we inhale chemical molecules from the air. These molecules stimulate sensory nerves located high in the nose. The nerve signal travels to a specific location in the brain called the *olfactory bulb*. These smell signals move directly on to the limbic system, which includes the amygdala and hippocampus. These areas of the brain process emotional responses such as anger, fear, happiness and love. They play a key role in making memories and storing them.

Smell and touch begin developing in the womb and are the most developed senses until adolescence. Studies indicate that newborn infants can identify their mother by scent! The smells experienced at a young age are closely linked to early childhood experiences and corresponding emotions. When we experience similar smells later in life, emotions linked with earlier times often are evoked.

FUN FACT

The allure of fragrances has been known since ancient times. Cleopatra reportedly used enticing oils to enhance her appeal. There is a wealth of knowledge regarding the positive impact of aromas on our psyches. The cosmetic industry has made a fortune by adding captivating scents to their products. Their chemists discovered that certain smells trigger the production of pheromones in the body, a chemical substance that can stimulate sexual attraction. The fragrances they've produced sell for a premium price.

NURTURING NATURE

To many, the chemical smell of sulfur reminds them of rotten eggs. But for me, the sulfuric smell of low tide immediately takes me back to the tidal pools of my childhood. I experience the glow of happiness accompanying the carefree feelings of my youth. For many, the smell of a freshly cut lawn brings them back to the halcyon days of summer.

Aromatherapy has been employed for centuries. Natural plant extracts called *essential oils* are used for therapeutic benefits. When inhaled, the scent molecules travel to areas of the brain controlling emotions. Various scents influence emotions in specific ways. Recent scientific studies have identified specific benefits of aromatherapy such as follows:

- Reduced anxiety and depression
- Headache relief
- Improved quality of sleep
- Boosted immunity

Many of the plants that provide therapeutic smells are common and easy to grow. Lavender is used to induce relaxation, relieve stress and anxiety, and promote sleep. Peppermint oil relieves tension and reduces headaches. Lemon balm is known as a mood lifter and calming herb. Like lavender, it reduces stress and anxiety and promotes sleep, along with improving appetite and easing indigestion.

While the application of essential oils requires a careful review of methods, doses, and potential side effects, simply smelling these plants has a soothing effect. As mentioned several times before, during the Cape Abilities garden tour, the participants always enjoy grabbing a fistful of lemon balm and mint to smell as we stroll along.

Chapter Three

The intoxicating aroma of flowers can evoke pleasurable memories.

The aromas of roses, lilies, and lilacs can be intoxicating, and many gardeners choose to grow them for their pleasurable scent. Other plants emit subtle smells, and you may only process them at an unconscious level. The fresh smell of pine trees comes from phytoncides. These are essential oils that activate an immune response in our bodies. Planting a stand of fast-growing cypress at the north border of the garden will not only provide a wind block to protect plants from the harsh north wind, but it will also bathe you in aromatic essential oils that boost your health!

Along with the health benefits of olfactory chemicals, many smells evoke happy memories. This is especially important for elderly populations. Many seniors live in confined environments with little opportunity to go outside and breathe in nature's fresh and healthful aromas. For the

> ### ☀ FUN FACT
>
> Lemon balm, a member of the mint family, is considered a calming herb. Dating back to the Middle Ages, it has been used to reduce stress and anxiety, promote sleep, improve appetite, and ease pain from indigestion.

Plants for Olfactory Pleasure

JASMINE: most fragrant flower

GARDENIA: a favorite perfume scent

HONEYSUCKLE: old-timey fragrance

LAVENDAR: soothing, pleasant smell

FREESIA: fruity scent

LILY OF THE VALLEY: one of the strongest aromas

ROSE: range from citrusy to a strong perfume aroma

HYACINTH: strong, sweet, earthy

SWEET PEA: strong, sweet fragrance

LILAC: intense scent

MOCK ORANGE: citrusy scent

TOBACCO PLANT: sweet, not like dried tobacco

ALYSSUM: sweet, subtle

MAGNOLIA: sweet

WHITE AND PINK PEONIES: sweet fragrance

HELIOTROPE: strong, sweet vanilla or fruity aroma

DIANTHUS: very fragrant, clove-like scent

PHLOX: sweet scent

SANTOLINA: pungent

Herbs

All herbs have unique and specific smells. The most distinct common herbs are basil, thymes, rosemary, cilantro, sage, dill, and chive. Creeping thymes can be planted between pavers for an aromatic walkway.

homebound, bringing a touch of nature inside, like fragrant flowers or a pot of herbs, might trigger happy memories from long ago. For those capable of jaunts outdoors, trips to an aromatic-rich garden will amplify the experience and provide the chance to walk down memory lane.

Vestibular Sensory System (Balance and More!)

Gardens offer a place for quiet reflection and immersion in the sensory world of aromas, sounds, and vibrant colors. The tasks involved in gardening tend to be slow-paced. Physical exertion is required, but flitting around is left to the butterflies and birds. Twirling around may occur on a movie set, with young lovers dancing in a rose garden, but in reality, most time spent gardening is fairly sedentary.

Although slow and steady, as we walk over an uneven surface or tip-toe between rows to avoid stepping on plants, our sense of balance is challenged. Balancing occurs thanks to the vestibular system, in conjunction with proprioception (body awareness) and kinesthesia (movement). Our ability to stand upright and move around without falling relies on this triad.

The "sense organ" for the vestibular system is located in the inner ear, and like hearing, it is complicated. The primary functions of the system are balance and detection of motion and speed. We instinctively know the position of the head, whether the head is tilted up or down, thanks to vestibular input. Vestibular stimulation affects the body in a multitude of ways:

- It has a pervasive influence on the overall processing of sensory information.
- It affects our gastro-intestinal function and heart rate.
- It charges up our muscle tone (especially in core muscles), getting us ready for action.
- It heightens general arousal states.

The vestibular system is activated through movement, such as rotation (spinning and rolling) and acceleration (speeding up or down). When we bend down, tilt our head, or move the head back and forth, we tweak the system as well. A healthy dose of vestibular input leads to improved muscle tone, general arousal, and connectedness to the world. When there is too much vestibular stimulation, we feel it in the gut. Normally, we are oblivious to vestibular input, but anyone who's experienced vertigo or motion sickness can attest to its powerful influence over our bodies.

For many of the neurodiverse children I have worked with over the years, activating the vestibular system through activities like swinging, spinning, and rolling has had a powerful therapeutic effect. Pete, for example, was a three-year-old non-verbal boy. He stared blankly into space with no visible affect. As I gently spun him around, his eyes came into focus and facial features brightened. Eye contact became consistent, and after a few sessions he began saying, "More," asking for another push to continue spinning. This was the spark that led to language and engagement in his world.

Chapter Three

While activities in the garden lack the wallop of vestibular stimulation that a rollercoaster provides, the calmer movements required still tweak this system. Bending over to weed or plant seeds tilts the head, which changes the position enough to get this system revved up. Turning back and forth from a wheelbarrow to shovel compost or mulch onto the garden bed requires head rotation. Repetition of these movements is like a gentle hum of stimulation. And the challenge of navigating through the garden activates balance responses.

Children, of course, will seek out vestibular stimulation at every turn. They may twirl, run, and hop around whenever given the opportunity. Providing outdoor spaces to engage in these healthy physical activities is key to healthy engagement in the world.

Activities to Activate the Vestibular System

- Bending down (tipping head downward): digging/weeding

- Turning head side to side: moving things like mulch/compost repeatedly

- Turning head for yes/no responses: group discussion during garden group

For the young (at heart?)

- Rolling in grass
- Summersaults
- Hopping and jumping
- Swinging

Vision

Years ago, health practitioners noticed that patients who had window views of trees recovered faster than those who didn't. Patients did not benefit from the production of vitamin D, because the window's glass blocked out the sun's UV rays. Situated inside on a hospital bed, there's no chance of inhaling those healthy aerosols from outside either. Something about the visual image of trees must have a healing effect on our bodies.

While personal and anecdotal accounts can attest to the pleasurable and often soothing effect of looking at mountains, ocean waves, and a stand of trees, scientists are beginning to uncover why these images evoke positive responses. Mid-twentieth-century mathematicians discovered fractals. Fractals are geometric shapes that display the same

Ferns are a perfect example of fractals:
The pattern repeats from the largest to the tiniest leaves.

characteristics as the whole. Similar patterns recur at progressively smaller scale. Mathematicians have developed theories to explain this. I prefer to look at examples like a branching tree to explain the phenomena. The pattern of the largest branches is replicated over and over, down to the tiniest twigs at the outermost reaches of the tree. Similarly, a fern frond's shape is repeated as the branches coming out of the main stem look like a miniature reproduction of the entire frond.

It's shocking to see how many unique fractals exist in nature. Some examples are as follows:

- Snowflakes
- Crystals
- Leaves of plants
- Pineapples
- River systems and tributaries
- Mountain ranges
- Lightning

Note that several of the "nature fractals" fascinate us, like looking at snowflakes and crystals and becoming awed by magnificent views. Which brings us back to the "Why?" Why do we love looking at these things?

Scientists have studied the way our eyes scan and interpret the world. The visual system is hardwired to understand certain fractal patterns, especially those occurring in nature. The visual cortex (the part of the brain that interprets visual information) feels most comfortable with natural features because humans have processed them throughout history. These visual images give rise to brain wave activity associated with relaxation and meditation. Levels of serotonin (the feel-good chemical) increase as well. So viewing a naturescape leads to a Zen-like

The captivating beauty of this small garden soothes and mitigates the hustle-bustle (and some may say stress) of Commercial St. in Provincetown.

state, which reduces stress. Decreased stress lowers cortisol levels in the blood, the chemical that wreaks havoc on our health. Smell a tree ... hug a tree ... it seems that simply looking at a tree might save us!

Throughout most of history, humans lived in rural settings. That shifted in this millennium. In 2008, humans officially became an '"urban species."' That means most people now live in urban areas. But the human's ability to evolve or adjust physiologically takes centuries. As a result, we need to adapt. Some posit that the dependency on chemicals (drugs and alcohol) and the increasing rise in stress-related illnesses have occurred, in part, due to this disconnect with nature.

Researchers studied people's responses to nature scenes, contrasting their responses with those viewing and walking in urban settings.

The group looking at city scenes did not experience the same health benefits as those who looked at nature scenes. Essentially, walking outside on a city street or looking at pictures of city scenes conjured up none of the stress-reducing benefits found in nature experiences. The complex, angular patterns found in cities are difficult to process, which leads to discomfort.

How does this tie into gardening? Gardens provide a bridge between wild, natural settings and more organized planning of the immediate outdoor environment. Fractal patterns can be found in many plants, while colors and varied shapes pique our attention.

Colors have been associated with emotional responses. Green is associated with health, and yellow with joy. The blue of the sky evokes a sense of spirituality, while colors in the red family burst forth with emotional energy like power.

Whether creating an English garden that appears random but pops with a variety of shapes, sizes, and colors, or planting carefully measured rows of vegetables, the visual images can bring comfort and joy.

The gardening process also provides the opportunity to build and/or hone visual skills. Earlier in the book, the "Hand-Eye Motor

FUN FACT

The Magic of Viewing Nature (as seen through Mobile EEG Studies):

When Scottish volunteers entered a park, their brain waves showed evidence of lower frustration and arousal, along with higher meditation levels. Essentially, walking in green spaces is restorative.

*Beauty can be found in cultivated landscapes like this
vineyard in Truro (Truro Vineyards, Truro, Massachusetts)*
Photo by Joe Navas/Organic Photography

Chapter Three

Children and adults become enthralled in observing the beauty of butterflies, both in stillness and when they take flight.

Coordination" section reviewed the way simple gardening tasks help develop the connection between eyes and hands. In essence, our vision guides our hands to work with resultant more accurate performance. Gardening also requires visual focus, which is the eye's ability to look intently at one point of interest, thus improving the ability to visually attend to specific things. Working with seeds and plantings also requires visual discrimination. Identification of a specific type of seed or seedling helps to refine this skill.

Another important visual skill is figure-ground visual discrimination. This especially comes into play when weeding. Being able to tell the difference between the weeds and the plants you want to nurture requires concentration and the ability to look at small details while scanning the larger visual field (the garden bed).

Many other things occur in the garden that tweak our visual attention and help build endurance in visually attending to things. In all the garden groups I have run, adults and children alike are fascinated as they observe butterflies and bees gathering nectar and pollinating

FUN FACT

The Potted Plant Study:

Researchers found that having plants in hospital rooms following surgery as compared to not having plants did the following:

- Shortened post-operative hospital stay
- Decreased use of pain medications and reports of pain
- Decreased reports of anxiety and fatigue

Simply having a potted plant in a room is restorative!

flowers. The insect movements are particularly mesmerizing because they stay relatively still for several moments, affording the ability to look at the patterned wings, the antennae, and other details of their anatomy. But sudden movements occur, leading to a different kind of visual attention, scanning a larger space to track their flitting movements. Observing butterflies and birds fly requires visual tracking. This is also a skill needed for reading.

Vision is the strongest sensory system for processing the world. We know that getting outside and immersing ourselves in nature has immense benefits. Simply walking outside in the sunshine helps with the healthy formation of the eyes and good vision, thanks to the sun's rays. Looking at nature, even something as simple as a potted fern, offers images that are comforting to the visual system and activates good vibes in the brain. Along with all the feel-good benefits of looking at nature and gardens, the action of gardening helps build visual focus and discrimination, critical for learning.

Chapter Three

Taste

No need to delve into any mathematical formulation or complex neu-rological explanations here. When we eat certain foods, the pleasure centers in the brain light up. Spoiled and toxic vittles lead to unpleasant physiologic responses, like gagging or vomiting. Mountains of literature review the benefits of certain food groups and the negatives of others. No need to litigate the nutritional pros and cons of the nightshades

Growing vegetables is a culinary delight, a source of pride and creative artistry.

versus legumes here, but few would argue with this assertion: Fresh homegrown food is delicious!

A tomato plucked from a vine and eaten within days simply tastes better than one that travels for many weeks in a container ship from Chile. I've witnessed children excited to fill a bag full of beans and cucumbers, as if they were grabbing a fistful of gummy bears. Gardening offers visual beauty, aromatic experiences, and soothing sounds. Cultivating plants requires physical engagement, which augments our emotional and physical well-being. But at the end of the day, the big prize is a basket full of nutritious and delicious food!

CHAPTER FOUR

Getting Started

Gardens can sprout anywhere from the tiniest urban spaces, to larger swaths of land. If you are a seasoned gardener, then you already know the time and energy required to turn tiny seeds into food and flora, and can plan accordingly. For the nascent gardener, begin small. Even one planter growing beans, lettuce, and cherry tomatoes will provide a sense of accomplishment and the thrill of eating food that you grow.

I began with a 10 ft. × 20 ft. box at our cottage on Cape Cod, after abandoning hope of growing food for my family on our wooded lot in Connecticut. The rapacious wildlife always beat me to the harvest. My new challenge: building healthy soil on a sandbar. As my soil improved, my harvest grew, and in a few years, I expanded to many raised beds. But if I'd attempted to start with ten sizeable beds, I would have quit, overwhelmed by the weeding, watering, feeding, and demands of a bountiful harvest.

Starting small can be just as rewarding as cultivating a huge plot.

What to Plant

There are four main considerations in planning a garden:

1. **Location:** geographic and immediate environmental factors
2. **Space:** determining whether to plant in pots, planters, raised beds, or plots of land, depending on the space you have
3. **Budget:** gardening from a shoe-string budget to high-end landscapes
4. **Objective:** determining what you want to grow given the above constraints

LOCATION

There are macro and micro considerations in the selection of plants to grow. If you live in a tropical climate, cold-loving crops like spinach will languish, while northern climates have short growing seasons, so certain heat-loving crops will not thrive. While you might love pineapples, there is zero chance of growing a pineapple grove successfully in Maine or Minnesota.

The US Department of Agriculture (USDA) has compiled a Hardiness Zone Map, based on the average minimum winter temperature. It is a guide to identifying plants that can survive and thrive in those conditions. There are eleven growing zones in the United States. The online map is very helpful. Type in your zip code, and it gives you your zone. For example:

- Raleigh, North Carolina: Zone 8A: Winter temperature range is 10 to 15 degrees Fahrenheit.
- Portland, Maine: Zone 6A: Winter temperature range is -10 to -5 degrees Fahrenheit.

You can also access the final frost date in the spring and the first frost date in the fall, which is critical to knowing when to plant outside and when to finish harvesting.

Another consideration is the immediate environment. Most plants need sunlight—the more, the better. Sunlight from the east, south, and west—preferably all three is ideal. If you only have north-facing exposure, you might consider plants that require less light. There are many shade-loving flowers, and a box of lettuce will thrive in dappled light.

Like humans, plants don't like stuffy conditions but get stressed out if constantly battered by gale-force winds. Locations that provide airflow but protect plants from the harshest winds do best. My garden sits high on a bluff, near the Atlantic's icy gale, so my garden tends to lag behind my fellow gardeners until the gentle summer breezes take over. But thanks to the continued airflow, I have fewer problems with fungal diseases than the folks with gardens well protected.

In urban settings, pots on a sunny windowsill or sunny corner of a room will thrive, as long as it's not too drafty. Balconies and porches afford even more space to experiment with. Rooftop gardens are becoming ever more popular.

How much space to cultivate depends on the amount of time and energy you want to invest. As mentioned earlier, small-scale gardening still reaps many benefits without the fatigue and frustration of a full-on garden. Here are small-scale solutions to get started:

- Pots of various sizes
- Plant grow bags
- Tubs
- Straw bales
- Small raised beds

Fast-growing decorative plantings can serve as a wind block.
This majestic display of broom grows wild on Cape Cod.

Chapter Four

This guide will provide tricks and strategies to minimize the work of maintaining the garden no matter what shape and size you decide to pursue!

BUDGET

You can go to a Home Depot or a boutique garden center and spend a fortune on pots and gardening supplies. Or you can dig into that old cupboard or closet and unearth a trove of unused cooking pots. Maybe drag out some storage boxes or plastic bins. If you're the tidy type and don't hoard forgotten and unused items, head to the local thrift shops, garage sales, and flea markets. You're bound to find a variety of shapes and styles of vessels.

After filling two raised beds with sweet potato plants, I found metal tubs at a flea market for a great price to plunk the remainder of my sweet potato slips into. Vintage and chic!

If you're ready to expand beyond small-container gardening, there are many intermediary options. Straw bales, plant grow bags, and whiskey barrels serve as good alternatives to garden plots with easy access and minimal maintenance.

Raised beds require an initial outlay of materials and labor, but once built, they last several years and require less maintenance than a garden plot. Digging up an area of the ground to cultivate may cost less if the soil is fairly healthy and does not require too many supplements. In one afternoon, you might have a completed garden plot. Over time, however, there tends to be more weeding, as unwanted vegetation has an easier time crawling into the bed.

You do not need to limit yourself to standard pots—be creative. Any vessel with drainage capabilities will work.

Soil is the one ingredient not to scrimp on. If you live in an area blessed with rich, friable soil, all you need to do is shovel, pull up the weeds, and add some compost, and you're good to go. But in this imperfect world, the terra firma we walk upon is not ideal and usually requires augmentation.

Surrounded by forest, my Connecticut garden benefited from centuries of leaf decomposition and resulting humus. I had perfect soil, except that thousands of years ago, glaciers slipped by, depositing unmitigated rock fields. Creating a garden was a time-consuming and laborious process. Shoveling the sandy soil at our Cape house is a dream come true, except sand does not provide the nutrients necessary to grow vegetables. I've spent years fortifying the soil, which now provides an abundant harvest.

Sourcing old wood creates a rustic look. (Shelburne Farms, Shelburne, Vermont)

Some wood, screws, a drill, metal corner brackets, and an extra pair of hands (or paws?) are all you need.

The planting begins!

NURTURING NATURE

The US Department of Agriculture has established a partnership with colleges and universities in most states to provide soil-testing services. If you plan on digging into the ground, it's a good idea to get the dirt analyzed. The analysis will let you know if you have the proper balance of nutrients and also identify toxins that sadly riddle much of our land.

If you're starting with containers or small raised beds, purchase organic soil and compost. Non-organic is cheaper, but do you want to feed your plants toxins that end up in the food you eat? Birds, bees, butterflies, and other animals ingest the toxins as well.

Compost is a key ingredient. Making your own is an option, but it takes time, so the first season, you will need to source the compost. Many municipalities have begun composting programs and provide residents with compost free of charge. If this is not available in your community, local nurseries sell organic compost. Depending on the amount you need, you can purchase bagged or bulk (by the yard). If you don't have a pickup truck, they will deliver for a fee.

Plants get hungry, especially as they're creating beautiful blossoms, fruit, foliage, and roots. So plant food is another necessary ingredient. The type of supplements depends on what you grow. There are generic types of fertilizer, and specific nutrients for various classes of food (for example, root vegetables like potatoes vs. leafy greens). Local nurseries can help guide you on specifics. Alternatively, doing an online search will list a slew of websites. Type the name of the plant and nutrient requirements into the search bar, and you'll find all the information you need.

Chapter Four

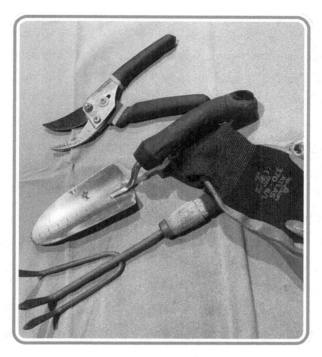

Pruner, trowel, hand rake and gloves are all you need to get started. Add a shovel, hoe, and garden rake, and you're all set!

It is tempting to grab the Miracle Grow or equivalent when you look at the price tag, but keep in mind that non-organic fertilizers contain toxins. Think baby formula. I couldn't understand how infants had ingested plastics, until I read that baby formula ingredients were grown with fertilizers encased in plastic for slow release into the soil. The crops gobbled up the plastic and turned it into an unwanted baby formula ingredient!

Once you get started, there are many ways to make your own compost and garden food. You will learn how later in the guide.

NURTURING NATURE

There are a few essential garden tools you will need. If you're sticking to small container gardens, a few old spoons of various sizes will do the trick. If you've chosen to create a larger garden, a few essentials are listed below:

- Shovel
- Trowel
- Garden fork (small-handheld)
- Gloves
- Rake
- Small pruner

For the budget conscious, many of these items can be found at tag sales. There is a wide range of pricing in retail purchases, but I have found my generic tools have served me well. I did not purchase top-of-the-line products ten years ago, but they still get the job done.

A water source is another essential for all gardens. Again, depending on the size of your garden, it can be as simple as saving water jugs to douse plants in their containers, or as extensive as a full-blown irrigation system. Generally, the first three items listed below are necessary:

- Watering can (long spout with removable sprinkler head)
- Hoses long enough to reach all parts of the garden
- Adjustable nozzles (shower, jet) for hose
- Irrigation (self-installed or professional installation)

If the garden is located at a facility such as a school or day care center, an irrigation system with a timer is helpful for the times when the facility is closed and there is no one there to water. An advantage of drip irrigation is that only the roots are watered. If the area you live in is prone to humid weather, keeping water off the leaves and fruit is a deterrent to mold and fungal diseases.

Chapter Four

Drip irrigation waters the roots while preventing
excess moisture that can lead to fungal diseases.

On the plus side of using a hose, while watering, you get to inspect the plants and identify weeds, invasive insects, and other potential problems. Literally, you can nip the problem in the bud. Watering can be a meditative experience. At one time, I practiced my yoga balancing poses as I watered the potato patch.

Watering is a favorite activity for students and the special needs populations I work with. There's little chance of making a mistake, and the plants are so grateful for a drink on those dry, sultry days!

 ## Prepping

Seeds are the most economical, and the magic of seeing a tiny seed transform into a thriving plant and produce flowers and food is amazing!

However, some plants have long growing cycles and do better planted as seedlings. Others require propagation from root cuttings and other methods.

Many communities have initiated seed-sharing programs. Local libraries frequently host these exchanges. After a successful growing season, you can harvest seeds and become self-sustaining. Gardeners like to share the bounty. Reach out to local garden clubs to see if they offer cutting or plants for free or at a discount. Farmers markets are good places to purchase seedlings in the spring and early summer. Friends who garden might have excess plants and be willing to share.

I have a tendency toward lassitude at the end of the growing season, so I allow some plants to go to seed rather than pulling everything up. Now that I have healthy soil, in the spring, those seeds turn into Asian greens, arugula, parsley, and more. They grow like weeds, so I offer many of these seedlings to friends and the community garden that I volunteer at. Be nosy and ask your gardening friends what they're growing. Ask for a tour. I promise, they love to talk about their vegetables and showcase their beautiful flowerbeds. And if they have excess, they're bound to share.

DECIDING WHAT TO GROW

After determining the budget, the amount of space and light you have, and what grows best in your geographic area, have fun dreaming about what you'd like to grow.

- Food!
- Beautiful flowers!
- A sensory extravaganza!
- Butterfly garden!

Chapter Four

Happily, these are not mutually exclusive. When my garden's parsley and dill begin to flower, butterflies flock there to drink the nectar. Flowers make excellent companions for food crops, bringing nutrients deep in the ground up toward the surface, making them available for fledgling vegetable seedlings to access. Many blossoms attract beneficial insects and draw pests away from food growing nearby.

Sensory gardens emphasize the textures, vibrant colors, and aroma of growing plants. The scarlet flowers of pole beans, lavender of sweet potatoes, which are in the morning glory family, and orange blossoms from squash plants provide vibrant colors. Brush against basil and cilantro, and the fragrance pops.

Success and simplicity may be the overall objective, so choosing easy-to-grow plants may be the way to go. If you're locked into an academic calendar, quick-growing spring crops and slow-growing plants that reach maturity in the fall are smart choices.

HOW TO PLANT

When to dig seeds into the ground and plant seedlings depends on your frost zone and the temperature requirements of the plant. Following these guidelines is critical. Eager beavers often jump the gun and start planting too early. Think about those teaser spring days, when we gambol outside, basking in the sunshine, trading a winter parka for a light sweater. And then the sleet, wind, and cold come roaring back. Few enjoy hanging out in such conditions. Plants agree.

Onions are cold tolerant, so early last spring I planted my most robust onion plants, tucking them into a deep layer of mulch. I placed a

Comfrey and borage have deep roots, which bring nutrients up in the soil, making it easier for your vegetables to access. They also attract beneficial insects like butterflies and bees. They are great companion plants for any garden!

light row cover over the bed for extra protection. Alas, these fine specimens shriveled in the cold. Many weeks later I planted the remaining onions. These flourished, while it took months for the early plantings to catch up. My onions sent a message loud and clear: WE DON'T LIKE THE COLD!

While you wait for the temps to climb, there are many tasks to accomplish. Prepping beds, acquiring mulch, and assembling equipment all make the planting and overall maintenance much easier over the growing season.

Fast & Easy-to-Grow Spring Plants	**Summer into Fall Crops**
Snow peas	Bean (bush and pole)
Spinach	Beets
Arugula	Carrots
Asian greens	Cucumbers
Scallions	Eggplant
Radish	Kale & chards (rainbow pretty!)
Cilantro	Alliums (onions & leeks)
	Squashes
	Peppers & tomatoes
	Herbs

PREPPING POTS

- Clean with soap and water. (This eliminates dirt, germs, leftover insects, and eggs.)
- Make sure there is drainage. (If no drainage hole, poke a few nail holes into the bottom of the vessel.)
- Source good-quality organic soil.
- Source organic fertilizer.

PREPPING BEDS

- Weed thoroughly, making sure to pull up the roots. The more you get rid of before planting, the less weeding you will need to do later.

- While weeding, be vigilant for pests. Grubs, slugs, and snails over-winter, burrowed deep in the ground. You might also find eggs. Toss all into the trash. (I give them to my chickens, which they consider a delicacy!)
- Add 2 inches of compost.
- If the soil needs amending, dig supplements in along with the compost and soil.
- Ideally, you want loose soil, so it's easy for water to get absorbed, roots to penetrate, and baby plants to poke through the soil to find the sun.
- Cover until time to plant. This keeps new weed seeds and insects from establishing a new home in the carefully tended bed. It also hastens the warming of the soil. There are a variety of covers, from light fabric floating row covers, to plastics in various colors and sizes. Local nurseries will advise on the best options. A frugal strategy is to break apart cardboard boxes and spread them over the garden beds. Worms love cardboard, and the garden loves worms!

 Planting!

One of the most common errors is to overplant, crowding the plants so they need to compete for food and water. Like a crowded room, the space becomes stuffy, making it a perfect environment for pathogens to thrive. The rule "Less Is More" applies here.

Think about a tomato seed. It measures approximately $1/8^{th}$ of an inch. With the proper conditions, the vine can soar to six to eight feet.

Chapter Four

The ratio of above-the-ground vine size to root mass is 1:1. That means the tomato plant needs to find equivalent space under the ground to set roots. Similarly, a sunflower left in a small pot will not grow five to six feet high, or whatever the package says. Without room to lay down lots of roots, the plant's growth will be stunted.

It takes discipline to follow the rules. When I had a 10 × 20 foot box, I stuffed so many plants in there, they were choking. The more I squeezed in, the less I harvested. Even in my expanded garden, I still struggle. I hate to discard living things, so I tend to tuck one more plant in here and there. Sure enough, when I do this, the yield declines. This is why I love sharing plants with friends, neighbors, and the community garden. Everyone wins, especially the plants!

Even though lettuce seedlings are tiny, they need space to grow. If planting for baby greens, you can plant close together, but if you want gorgeous big heads, make sure you give plenty of space.

PLANTING SEEDS

- Follow recommended spacing and depth.
- Cover with soil, then gently pat to make the soil firm but not too compact.

- Water with a gentle spray (too hard will disrupt the placement of the seed).
- Mulch.

An entire crop grows on the dining room table. After hardening out for a few weeks, they're ready to get planted.

PLANTING SEEDLINGS AND TRANSPLANTS

- Follow recommended spacing.
- Carefully remove from pot.
- Loosen roots. (Don't plant with bunched-up root ball.)
- Place in a pre-dug hole, making sure all roots are covered.
- Pat firmly so the plant is secure.
- Mulch.
- Keep watered.

Chapter Four

Mulch Options

Organic

Shredded dried leaves

Dried grass clippings

Salt marsh hay

Eel grass

Straw (Chopped is easiest to work with. Do NOT use HAY, since it contains seeds that sprout, leading to constant weeds!)

Inorganic

Landscape fabric

Black plastic (Warms soil in spring, but might be too hot in summer. Requires special watering: either drip irrigation or direct flow to the plant, as water does not go through plastic materials.)

Eel grass is the perfect mulch ... and it's free!

Growing

If you've been diligent in weeding and mulching, there shouldn't be too much work during the growing season. However, weeds are persistent devils, and they find a way into the most protected gardens. Ditto pests! So, weeding on a regular basis keeps them from taking over. When you see a weed, yank it up. The sooner, the better ... Weeds left in the ground spread roots, bear seeds, and spread.

Add more mulch as the season progresses to stifle opportunities for weeds to take root.

FEEDING

Plants require more nutrition just as they set fruit and continue to produce. Look at the requirements for each specific plant, but the rule of thumb is as follows:

- Feed as blossoms appear.
- Top-dress with one inch of compost halfway through the season.
- Feed monthly with an organic fertilizer.

INSECT CONTROL

The first line of defense in keeping insects at bay is ensuring the health of the plant. Healthy plants send out a chemical code: "Don't mess with me." On the other hand, like in humans with a weakened immune system, pathogens take hold faster when the plant is unhealthy. In essence, insects can detect weakness and take full advantage. Keeping your plants well-fed and hydrated deters those nasty predators.

Mulching also limits the number of critters that burrow into the soil. But pests can be tenacious and find ways to creep in, especially when you're growing such delectable food!

COMBATING SLUGS, GRUBS, AND SNAILS

- Diatomaceous earth (DE): Made from organic crushed fossils, DE scrapes the tender bodies of these unsavory characters, so they avoid plants that have this powder sprinkled on and around them.
- Beer traps: Yup, they like beer. They'll crawl into a strategically placed cup dug into the soil, and drown.
- Search and capture: Especially early morning or evening. Look under pots and around your plants.
- Eliminate hiding places: Make sure it is weed-free around garden beds.

WORMS, APHIDS, AND INSECT EGGS

- Search and collect, especially the underside of leaves and tender new shoots.
- Use BT (*Bacillus thuringiensis*) an organic bacteria that gives insects a tummy ache but doesn't affect humans.

OTHER PESTS

My garden resembles Fort Knox. The rabbits slip right through the wire fencing, so each raised bed is individually fenced with a fine mesh material. Floating row covers prevent birds from stealing seeds that have just been planted. Keeping the row cover on until the plants germinate has increased my yield significantly.

Paradoxically, having birds flitting around the garden helps later in the season. Their eagle eyes spot tomato worms and snatch them off before the worms burrow into the fruit. Turkeys, on the other hand, can be a real disaster. My dog guards against the turkeys that frequently visit. Millie's favorite pastime is chasing the fowl as they gobble their way up to rooftops and trees to escape.

Rodents, like chipmunks, mice, and voles, dig their way into almost anything. Usually they're after insects, but inadvertently disrupt roots. Chipmunks especially love to eat what we eat. Many gardeners spend a lifetime trying to outwit Alvin and his friends. Some have come up with inventive solutions, which are too unkind to write about here. Sometimes you have to resign yourself to sharing the bounty with your four-legged neighbors.

Harvest

Barring a terrible infestation of pests or a natural disaster, if you follow the steps outlined in this chapter, you should reap a bountiful harvest. In the garden groups that I help out with, each participant goes home with a goody bag of veggies or a bouquet of flowers. If this is a family enterprise, imagine the joy of walking into your yard or onto your porch to get the ingredients for dinner!

CHAPTER FIVE

A Year of Garden Activities

PEA SHOOTS (WINTER)

Who says that growing ends with the winter solstice? Pea seeds germinate fast and can be grown for microgreens in large open trays. It takes only a few weeks for the seedlings to grow. When they reach six inches, you can snip off the stems in bunches. They can be eaten raw, adding pizzazz to a salad, or used in stir-fries.

 Equipment:

- Organic potting soil
- Large waterproof bin
- Pea seeds (Place seeds in glass jar and soak in water for 24 hours for faster germination.)

- Water
- Large spoon to stir soil and water
- Plastic trays (Saved plastic containers can be substituted as long as the sides are 3 inches high.)
- Newspaper to line trays
- Garden labels (craft popsicle sticks work) and permanent marker
- Plant sprayer

Directions:

1. Dump potting soil into bin (fill about halfway).
2. Gradually add water. Keep stirring to make sure all the water is fully absorbed. The consistency of the soil when done should be spongy.
3. Line trays with several layers of newspaper if they have holes in them.
4. Scoop soil from bin and dump into trays. Fill to top of trays.
5. Soil should be spread evenly over the top.
6. Pea seeds are placed over the entire surface area, and then soil is sprinkled on top of the seeds to completely cover them.
7. Gently pat the soil over each tray once the seeds are covered.
8. Place trays on windowsills and water daily.
9. As plants emerge, they can be measured.
10. When shoots reach approximately 6 inches, cut off and enjoy!

Benefits:

- Working with soil is a tactile activity, helping to acclimate those sensitive to touch and allowing sensory-seeking children the opportunity to have a touch-immersion experience.

Pea seeds in tray & pea shoots growing]

- The rapid growth of pea seeds gives ample opportunity to observe how seeds convert to a living plant and an opportunity to teach the plant's life cycle.

FUN FACT

Mycobacterium vaccae is a microbe found in soil. This bacterium has a similar effect on neurons that antidepressants like Prozac provide. It may stimulate serotonin production, which makes you happy. These antidepressant microbes are also being investigated for improving cognitive function, Crohn's disease and rheumatoid arthritis.

Take away: Play in the dirt to improve your mood and life!

SEED BOMBS

When forests were destroyed by wildfire, reseeding and planting all the crags and crevices of mountainous terrain posed a significant challenge. Some brilliant individual came up with the idea of sticking seeds into little clay balls and tossing them strategically from an airplane. The ball is heavy enough to get pulled to earth (while seeds alone have the potential to fly for miles beyond the targeted locale). Compost and soil are mixed into the clay orb so all the nutrients required upon landing are present for the seeds to germinate and grow.

Flower bombs are the ammunition of choice in *guerrilla farming*. Folks walk around the city, and when they encounter an abandoned lot or other such eye sore, they toss their seed bombs. Our kids bring flower bombs home to beautify their yards.

 Equipment:

- Clay (natural, not plasticine)
- Native seeds
- Tiny cups (such as pill cups) to hold seeds
- Compost
- Soil

☀ *FUN FACT*

Touch operates on two systems: protective and discriminatory.

We need both, but sometimes the protective system takes over and hypersensitivities result. Clay is an excellent material to help people overcome their discomfort with touching unfamiliar textures.

Chapter Five

Directions:

1. Presort seeds into cups (we gave a mini-cup to each child).

2. Roll out small clay balls.

3. Work in soil and compost by pressing, rolling, and kneading.

4. Press seeds into the outside of the ball (approximately 6 per ball).

5. Place on a tray to dry (at least 24 hours).

Benefits:

- Increases hand strength and fine motor development.
- Opportunity for tactile exploration. Have a cloth and sink at the ready and assurance that hand washing is available after making the seed bomb.

CHOOSING SEEDS AND MAKING A PLAN

Every January, my mailbox gets stuffed with seed catalogs. In this digital age, when practically everything we want is a click away, few remember the thrill of receiving the three-inch-thick catalog from Sears and Roebuck or Montgomery Ward in the mail. Even though everything can be ordered online, as the wind roars and temperatures plummet, perusing the colorful pages of the seemingly endless seed catalogs is a balm. Getting outside and absorbing the sun's rays is a distant dream. But thinking about seeds and growing plants provides an anchor and hope.

Did you know there are more than two hundred varieties of lettuce? You have the existential choice: grow heirloom tomatoes and beans to emulate relatives of long ago, or go for the blockbuster hybrids that promise a fabulous yield. How tall do you want your sunflowers? Do

Just looking at pictures of beautiful vegetation can make us happy!
(Butchart Gardens, Brentwood Bay, British Columbia)

you want a dramatic stand towering with single stalks and one giant flower, or branching with multiple blooms to cut and have beautiful bouquets?

So a fun activity in the dark days of winter is to leaf through catalogs, make lists, compare prices, and eventually order. (Yes, the companies usually have an easy online option to actually order the merchandise.) Ultimately, in the final selection, you are limited by logistics and geographic constraints, but deep in the winter months, have fun imagining the possibilities.

 Equipment:

- Seed catalogs (If not on mailing lists, visit online sites. Most have an option to send catalogs in the mail.)
- Paper and pencils
- Blank paper or graph paper to sketch out the garden plan

Chapter Five

Directions for Garden Groups:

1. Collect multiple catalogs so everyone has their own to circle or tear out pictures of desired plants.

2. Brainstorm: have a discussion of preferences. (For example: "What do you like to eat?" ... "French fries." ... "Great, let's grow potatoes!")

3. Create a list of possible plants.

4. Curate: discuss what is actually possible given the garden constraints.

5. If the list is still long, take a vote. (Ask each member to write down 1–3 choices on individual index cards. Tally responses.) OR take a straw poll. ("Raise your hand if you want tomatoes ... peppers ..." and so on.)

6. Sketching out a garden plan with the layout requires calculating the amount of space available and the space requirements of each plant. This requires higher-level skills that might be best done by the garden coordinator, or a member of the group who may have this particular skill set.

If this endeavor is a family effort, you can still follow these steps, but scale down decision-making to a more informal process.

Benefits:

- Visually enjoyable activity
- Taps into planning and making long-term goals
- Group interaction and discussion

MAKING COMPOST

Why bother? In 2022, US landfills acquired 146.1 million tons of trash. Processing one household's organic waste will hardly make a dent in the mountains of trash. But tossing spoiled vegetables and coffee grounds into a small bin turns into liquid gold for your garden. The nutrients of finished compost add a powerful punch to the soil used for growing flowers and vegetables.

When I began composting kitchen scraps, trips to the dump were cut in half. I keep a gallon-sized container under the sink and empty it to the outside composter every couple of days. Each year, I end up with many wheelbarrow loads to supplement the garden beds.

If you live in an apartment with no outdoor storage spaces, your options are limited. A small galvanized can or plastic tub with a tight lid in a size you can accommodate will work and provide enough compost to top-dress small pots. With a garage, shed, or yard, you have many options.

Chapter Five

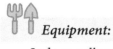

Equipment:

- Indoor collection vessel (any covered container will do)
- Outdoor composter (many varieties to choose from)
- Large composting piles (framed by scrap wood or fencing)
- Pitchfork, hoe, and shovel
- Screen sifter
- Gloves
- Large bucket or wheelbarrow to transport finished compost to garden pots and beds
- Soil thermometer (if you want to keep track of how hot/active your pile gets)

Inside composters

Composters come in many shapes and sizes. A screen, small hoe, and shovel are all you need to make your own compost.

In this large compost pile, note the green plant growing from discarded potatoes. Along with the compost, some potatoes will be harvested!

Directions:

- Collect food scraps and other compostable materials.
- When the indoor container gets full, transport contents to the outside composter.
- Make sure the compost pile outside remains moist.
- Stirring or turning the pile hastens the process.

Directions for Large Outdoor Piles:

1. Select a location not too far from the garden where you can build a compost pile. A shady location is ideal to maintain moisture in the heap.

2. Collect compost ingredients from your property (fallen aged leaves, grass clippings, dead plants).

3. Layer the ingredients, alternating greens* and browns.* Make sure everything dumped into the pile is moist. In between these layers, add a thin layer of grass clippings, finished compost, and/or soil to help activate the microorganisms that will feed on the "food."

4. Aged animal manure, if available, provides a big helping of nitrogen. (Alpaca, sheep, and chicken poops are cherished by farmers. If you can source this from local farmers who use organic practices, go for it!)

5. The smaller the bits going into the pile, the faster they will break down. So, chopping up leaves and grass with a mower and cutting up branches and food scraps before dumping them in the compost, will provide you with finished compost sooner.

6. Once you've layered the pile, mix the ingredients every couple of weeks. Turning the material stimulates microbial activity.

7. If you have an animal problem (rodent, raccoon), consider keeping an enclosed compost bin for the fresh foods, and once rotted, incorporate it into the open pile.

8. Patience! Depending on weather conditions, moisture, airflow, ingredients, and how diligently you've stirred the pile (or not!), the compost will be ready anywhere from 6 months to 2 years.

9. When most of the material has decomposed, shovel onto a screen and then sift back and forth with a hoe to get the finished compost into a bucket or wheelbarrow. Deliver to the desired location.

* *Greens:* nitrogen source that is colorful and wet (grass, coffee grounds, plant trimmings, eggshells, seaweed, manures)

* *Browns:* carbon source that provides structure and food to the pile (dead leaves, pine needles, twigs, straw, sawdust, corn stalks, paper, lint, cotton)

Compost Ingredients

Weeds*

Plant debris

Shredded/aged leaves

Grass clippings

Small quantities of wood shavings

Vegetable waste

Cut flowers

Foods: tea/bags, coffee grounds/filters, rinsed eggs shells, herbs, moldy food

Farmyard manures

Seaweed

Pet dander

Untreated paper products

Make sure roots are dead and there are no seeds

Compost No–Nos!

- Diseased plant materials, weeds with seeds, or live roots
- Animal kitchen waste (meats)
- Dog and cat manures
- Dairy products, fats and oils, sugars and salty foods, vinegar products
- Sticky tags from fruit
- Woody matter not cut into bits/shredded

Material Options to Construct an Open Bin

- Wire mesh/fencing
- PVC
- Recycled wood pallets
- Burlap (Local coffee roasters often have burlap bags for free.)

Sample Compost "Recipes"

- Equal parts manure and damp straw
- 3 parts grass clippings, 1 part kitchen scraps, 1 part damp straw
- 3 parts grass clippings, 1 part kitchen scraps, 1 part moist shredded paper

This is a brief introduction to composting. Refer to "Resources" in the back of the book for more extensive instructions.

Benefits:

- Enhances the garden by increasing the organic content of the soil, which improves drainage, increases fertility, adds nutrients, supports beneficial life forms in the soil, and helps plants resist pests and diseases.
- Cuts down on the trips to the dump or the necessity of a garbage service, along with contributing to a reduction of trash going into landfills.
- Provides simple activities such as shredding paper, chopping up food to go into the bin, and carrying the smaller indoor composter to the outside composting site.
- Provides heavy work activities along with strengthening muscles, which activate filters in the brain, thereby helping to reduce anxiety and calm individuals.

FUN FACT

According to the Environmental Protection Agency (2018) Municipal Solid Waste totaled 292.4 million tons (that's 584,800,000,000 pounds!)

They calculate that the average American produced approximately 5 pounds a day. The breakdown is: food: 21.6 percent, paper products: 23 percent, and yard trimmings: 11.4 percent.

This means approximately 56 percent can be composted.

NURTURING NATURE

WORM FARMS

Each year, the Truro Children's Community Garden group selects an animal theme. They learn about how the animal contributes to nature and the health of the garden. In past years they've chosen chickens (they provide poop/aka fertilizer), bees (are super pollinators), goats (eat the weeds). One year they chose earthworms. Along with learning how vital these creepy crawlers are to the health of the soil, surprisingly, many of the kids became ardent fans. Children who hated gooey things learned to hold and protect them. When finding worms as they worked the soil, they made sure the worms didn't get injured. A few boys talked about how cute they were and would run back to the garden to say goodbye to their creeping friends before they went home.

Earthworms transform rotting organic material into compost. The worm castings, or vermicompost, help the growth of the plants and assist in improving the soil.

Earthworms help out in the following ways:

- Improve soil physically by making tunnels that help air, water and plant roots move through the soil.
- Improve soil chemically by transferring decomposing organic matter into nutrient-rich tidbits that serve as plant food. These chemicals help the plants' resistance to root rot, improve the germination rate, and promote robust root growth.
- The castings are high in nitrogen, phosphorous, calcium, and iron.
- Nightcrawlers (the big guys) push organic matter deep into the soil to the root zone of plants, making it easier for the plant to absorb nutrients.

Chapter Five

While starting a worm farm is hardly a substitute for our furry friends, minimal care once started results in rich plant food to augment your planters and garden beds! A fifteen-gallon plastic bin produces approximately five gallons of vermicompost every four to five months.

 Equipment:

- Container: Plastic bin (12 gallons or larger), drill (1/4 inch drill bit), or hammer with nails to make small holes scattered between the sides (lower half: 6 inches apart, top half: 4 inches apart). This is for airflow. Alternatively, you can purchase a worm farm kit. (See "Resources.")
- Rubber gloves: For working in the materials.

Prepping the Worm Bin:

1. Tear 2- to 3-inch strips of newspaper and dunk in a bucket of water. This carbon-rich layer should fill approximately half of the bin.
2. Move the bin to the permanent location, as it will get heavy with the next ingredients.
3. Top off this layer with compost (4 cups) and soil (2 cups), making sure these are *not* chemically treated or sterile. These ingredients provide beneficial bacteria and microbes, adding nutrition for the worms.
4. Add plain cornmeal (2 cups).
5. With a spray bottle, water each layer and work in with gloved hands. Spritz until everything is uniformly moist, but not overly wet.

6. Once the bin is prepped, worms* can be added. (See "Resources.") Gently place the worms inside. Divide rotting vegetable and fruit scraps into four portions and bury them 1–2 inches deep in the bedding.

7. Place top on the bin.

8. After a few days, stir up and mix again. Spritz any areas that seem dry.

9. Gather kitchen scraps and feed up to 3 times a week. Toss into the bin and cover with a layer of brown matter (like a few pages of yesterday's newspaper). Keep closed in between additions of food. Make sure the material stays moist by using a spray bottle.

* For best results, purchase worms. There are 2,500 species of earthworms. While you can harvest worms from your yard, to get started, it's best to source your first batch commercially, as they have cultivated varieties that specialize in the decomposition of waste matter.

 Directions for Ongoing Care:

1. Prep the worm bin as described above, or if purchasing a commercially made worm farm, follow the instructions provided.

2. Keep the worm farm in a cool, dry place, such as a shed, garage, or basement. The most productive temperature is between 55 and 75 degrees. Keep covered except when feeding and amending the bedding materials.

3. Feed three times weekly *(If food is consumed quickly, feed more often)*. Non-citrus fruit, seed-free vegetable scraps, cleaned eggshells, soy products, tea bags, coffee grounds, nuts, seeds, nut shells, human and pet hair, laundry lint, rice, pasta, non-dairy baked goods, grass clippings, seedless weeds.

4. Do not give citrus, avocado rinds, pickled and salty foods, vinegar, dairy products, alliums, hot peppers, cabbage family, eggs, meat, bones, pet feces, cat litter, plastics, wood, charcoal ash, sand, diseased plants, fats, grease.

5. Periodically check to make sure the materials are moist but not wet. Signs of excess water include worms congregating in corners or crawling up the walls of bin and mold forming. If this occurs, add rolled-up newspaper and tuck several inches below to absorb excess water. Wipe away any mold forming. Keep the top off with the light on for a while to help reduce moisture. (The worms don't like the light, so they won't try to escape.)

 Directions for Harvesting and Vermiculture Use:

New worm farms may take up to six months to create a robust yield of worm castings. You can snitch some along the way or wait for the big harvest. Here's a method to harvest all at once:

1. Transfer worm-laden vermicompost into a bucket. Place in good light so the worms will migrate to the bottom of the bucket (not liking light!).

2. Wait two hours, then scoop out the top layer and place in a colander.

3. Castings are 75 percent moisture, so fit the colander inside a bucket to catch the liquid. The liquid collected can be stored in a container and used as compost tea during the growing season.

4. Fluff occasionally.

5. After a few days, most of the moisture should be gone from the vermiculture, but it should not be completely dry. Sift through and

gently break up any remaining clods. Store in a container that provides some airflow. (Punch a few holes if necessary.)

6. Worm castings are a great addition to potting soil—it's like a high potency vitamin. The ratio should be no more than 20 percent of the soil mixture.

7. Top dress ¼-inch layer for houseplants. Side dress growing plants in the garden.

8. When planting, dig a hole for a plant and put a handful of vermiculture into the hole before placing the plant in.

 Benefits:

- Great activity to help tactile-sensitive individuals cope with unfamiliar textures.
- Generates essential nutrients for the garden (worm-casting compost and tea).
- Uses waste in a beneficial way rather than contributing to landfills.
- Provides many repetitive tasks that can be accomplished easily during the setup: tearing up newspaper, spraying, scooping in materials, mixing with gloved hands.
- Provides easy tasks such as cutting or tearing food into smaller bits so it gets processed faster and accelerates the composting process.
- Provides sorting tasks such as sorting out food scraps by having a food chart with foods that the worm can eat.

FUN FACT

Earthworms have assisted in the clearing of polychlorinated biphenyls (PCBs), which are cancer-causing compounds.

In an Indiana study, scientists placed red worms in a toxin-laced area. *After 200 days the worms had removed 80 percent of the PCBs in the soil!*

MAKING SIGNS

When the growing season begins, the flurry of chores can seem overwhelming. Weeding, hauling compost and mulch, hardening off seedlings, the list goes on and on. So once you plunk the seeds and plants in the ground, you're ready for a break. When the tall iced tea and a shady place to rest beckon, staying in the hot sun to identify beds seems tedious, if not downright annoying.

But in the winter, when you are itching to get going, you can channel the energy into making signs for the crops you grow. Vegetables and flowers are easy to draw, so most anyone can succeed at this task!

Equipment:

- Paints (tempera or acrylic)
- Paint brushes
- Wood shingles and shims (source leftovers from construction projects if possible)
- Hammer and nails
- Varnish

NURTURING NATURE

Directions:

1. Cover worktable with newspaper to catch dripping paint.

2. Make a list of the plants and have group members choose what they want to draw.

3. You can offer pictures or actual vegetables as models, or you can talk about what the plant looks like (tomato: red circle, bean: green line, carrot: skinny orange triangle).

4. Adding the written name is optional but not essential. Specific labels are made to identify specific varietals once you have the seed packets and seedlings. That's a separate activity explained later in the guide ("Making Labels for Every Plant").

5. Paint the wood (shingle) with words, pictures, and/or designs.

6. After the paint dries, paint varnish on. Varnish has toxins, so this might be a job for the garden leader rather than group participants.

7. After the paint and varnish dry, nail the wood shingle to a 1-inch wood shim.

8. Review all safety precautions necessary when using tools.

9. Provide close supervision as the nailing and hammering proceed!

Benefits:

- The drawing and painting use fine and visual motor skills.
- Tool use requires hand-eye motor coordination.
- Taps into creativity and pride in producing artwork.
- Adds an artistic dimension to the garden.

Chapter Five

 Spring

WEEDING (SPRING)

"Many hands make light the work." This especially applies to prepping the garden at the beginning of the growing season. Weeding is a terrific group activity. When clearing out an area, simply designate plots for each group member to do. If there are plants in the ground to work around, have individuals with good discrimination work in that vicinity, or demarcate a barrier around plants to be preserved.

While many view weeding as a tedious and laborious task, I find it meditative. Active meditation is "meditation in motion," focusing on a specific repetitive task. As I become absorbed in yanking out weeds, seeing, smelling, and feeling the soil makes nagging thoughts and worries melt away. Active meditation is highly effective in calming the mind and reducing anxiety. Along with the meditative effect of weeding, seeing an area cleared of weeds and ready for planting is a highly rewarding experience!

 Equipment:

- Garden gloves
- Trowel
- Hand tiller
- Bin
- Markers (if staking out specific areas to weed)
- Optional: kneel pads (kneeling cushions)

Directions:

1. Note the area to be weeded and identify the weeds. This is easy in the spring when most if not all of the bed is to be weeded.

2. If there is a mix of plants to remain in the ground, for example, perennial herbs, be sure to mark off the area to be preserved from the area to be weeded. You might use sticks or string to mark off the designated area to pull up weeds.

3. If the ground is hard, rake with a hand fork (tiller) or dig with a trowel to break up the soil.

4. Use garden gloves to pull up weeds. For deeply rooted plants, use the trowel to excavate. Try to get most of the root system, not just the tops of the plant.

5. Place refuse into a bin to discard.

6. If weeds are non-invasive without seeds, after the plants die off, they can be added to the compost pile. Otherwise, toss in the trash.

7. A pad to kneel on makes it easier to work.

8. The more thorough the early season weeding is, the less work there is throughout the season. Once the bed is completely prepped and plants are in the ground, a heavy layer of mulch will suppress most weeds during the season while also keeping the soil moist.

Many hands make weeding a snap!

Benefits:

- Increased hand strength and fine motor development.
- This is a real visual discrimination activity: first identifying the plants growing in the ground, then discriminating between weeds and desired plants.
- Weeding is repetitive and can be an active meditation, which calms the mind.

PREPPING THE GARDEN

Whether you plan on shoveling out a plot in the ground, making raised beds, or using containers and pots, prepping is key to successful growing. As I've mentioned, our home in Connecticut had beautiful soil, but since it was in the path of a glacier, it took hours to clear a small plot due to all the rocks. Now, living at the tip of Cape Cod, less than an inch below the surface, we have sand, as pure as the sand on the beach. So I've spent years amending the soil. In many locales, it's the opposite problem: soil heavy with clay. You can go to a local nursery to discuss your situation. If you want to get very serious and scientific, you can reach out to your state center for agriculture, sending soil samples to be tested, and they will send back a report of the amendments that need to be made. If you choose raised beds and containers, the solution is easy: Fill up with organic topsoil and compost.

Equipment:

- Organic potting soil
- Compost

- Shovel
- Trowel
- Hand tiller (Mini-rake)
- Wheelbarrow or buckets to haul soil/compost

 Directions for Garden Plots:

1. Using a shovel, dig up approximately 8–12 inches. Sift through to get rid of rocks, grass roots, and any other vegetation. Loosen the soil.
2. Rake through, making sure there are no clumps. Look for any bad insects (grubs, beetles, slugs, cutworms). Rescue and keep worms, the garden's best friend. Spiders eat bad bugs, so they can stay around too.
3. If the soil requires augmentation, work into the existing soil with a hand tiller or, if a large plot, a garden rake.
4. Top dress with 2 inches of compost.

 Directions for Pots and Containers:

1. Make sure the container is clean.
2. Add organic soil.
3. Top dress with 1–2 inches of compost.

 Benefits:

- Lots of physical activity: Use of shovels and rakes requires bilateral motor coordination and strength.
- Picking out weeds, rocks, and bad insects requires visual attention and visual discrimination.

Chapter Five

IDENTIFICATION: MAKING LABELS FOR EVERY PLANT

In the hustle and bustle of planting, it's easy to mix up the seedlings. Even experienced gardeners will have difficulty identifying a Brandywine tomato from a Big Beef slicer. To avoid confusion, prior to planting seeds and transplanting, make sure you have plenty of labels. You can purchase plastic markers in bulk or use popsicle sticks. Save the seed packets to have easy reference of what you've planted.

While you wait for the soil to warm up and the chilly air to abate, this is a perfect indoor group activity. Use the seed packets as a reference, or copy down the names on index cards. Each person can choose one plant name to copy onto a marker. Estimate the number of pots you will have and provide an equal number of markers. For some, copying the names may require concentration. For others, it won't require that much thought, so it becomes a good time for socializing while working.

 Equipment:

- Markers (plastic, craft popsicle sticks)
- Waterproof permanent markers
- Index cards or seed packets with names clearly marked
- Envelopes to store labels until planting time

FUN FACT

Shoveling and hauling are heavy work activities!

These activate the proprioceptive system in our bodies, which activates filters in the brain. That's one of the reasons we feel better after exercising.

Hauling compost is a favorite activity of pre-adolescent students—all that heavy lifting calms them down!

NURTURING NATURE

Directions:

1. List each type of seed you have planted with the name. (For example: Romaine Lettuce, Boston Bibb Lettuce, Cherry Tomato, Big Beef Tomato, Jalapeno Pepper, Bell Pepper).

2. Estimate how many seedlings you plan on transplanting of each variety.

3. Copy name on an index card for easy referencing to copy onto markers.

4. Distribute index cards to group members. (You may ask their preference, or decide the skill level of each individual and assign accordingly. For example, Pea is easier to write than Zucchini!).

5. Use waterproof permanent markers. You may place a pad or paper underneath so the marker doesn't mark up the table surface.

6. If you plan on having a dozen of each plant, be sure to create 12 markers per plant. (Depending on the skill level and stamina, you may need to divvy up by making multiple index cards with the plant name. For example, if writing tomato three times is a challenge, make 4 index cards with Tomato and assign 4 members of the group to create three labels each. Call them The Tomato Team.)

7. When completed, gather the markers and save them in an envelope to use when you pot the seedlings.

Benefits:

- This is an opportunity to practice writing. For those who have mastered this skill, it is an opportunity to demonstrate their proficiency.

- This is a great group activity. The level of conversation can be determined by the individual group member's need to concentrate on the task. Before and after the labels are made, discuss the plants and garden plans.

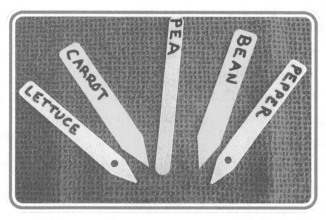

It's easy to confuse and forget what you planted, so making labels for individual plants is important ... and is a great group activity.

PLANTING SEEDS INSIDE

Your crew has fantasized about a perfect garden, come up with a plan, and winnowed the selection of seeds. When the seed packets arrive, sort them into two piles: those that will be directly seeded in the garden and those that need a head start by planting inside. The packets provide recommended planting methods. With longer growing seasons, warmer climates afford the opportunity to plant many seed varieties in the ground. For instance, spinach will grow throughout the winter in warmer climates. In areas with shorter growing seasons, you can start seeds indoors.

Plants like tomatoes and peppers take a long time to grow and require warm temperatures. Many gardeners choose to purchase seedlings at the nursery. For people like me, who itch to get working the soil by March, starting seeds inside gets the season rolling! There are many advantages:

- Economical: Seed packets cost a fraction of what seedlings cost at a nursery.
- Greater variety: Most nurseries have a limited number of choices of each type of plant. By ordering seeds, you get to choose between organic, heirloom, and a plethora of choices. (Remember: over 200 kinds of lettuce!)
- You have control of the conditions and nutrients the plant receives (organic rather than synthetic fertilizers and grow mediums, no pesticides).
- It provides the opportunity to observe the full life cycle of the plant and experience the thrill of seeing seeds germinate and grow into fruit- and flower-producing plants!
- It's a great kick-off to gardening groups and programs.

 Equipment:

- Organic seed starter soil/growing medium
- Large waterproof bin, bowl, or bucket
- Seeds
- Water
- Gloves
- Stirring device such as a large spoon

- Plastic trays
- Containers at least 2 inches deep with drainage (plastic flats, cell packs, recycled plastic containers—lettuce clam shells work especially well)
- Tray large enough to hold containers to catch drainage
- Plastic lid or plastic wrap
- Newspaper to catch soil mixture that doesn't make it into the planting container
- Garden labels (craft popsicle sticks work) and permanent marker
- Spray bottle
- Optional: heated grow mat
- Optional: broad-spectrum grow lights

Seed planting supplies

 Directions:

1. Wash containers thoroughly with soapy water.

2. Spread out newspaper in the work area to prevent mess and collect soil for re-use.

3. Spoon soil into trays/containers, leaving ½ inch from top. Press soil firmly so there are no air pockets.

4. Add seeds—try to space evenly. This gives seedlings a chance to form root systems.*

---

* Try to select larger seeds for individuals with poor dexterity and/or eyesight. Alternatively, scattering seeds randomly still works. Once the seedlings grow to two inches, they can be divided and placed in separate cells. This procedure is explained in "Potting Up Presents."

5. After planting seeds, sprinkle a very fine layer of the dry mixture on top of the seeds to cover them, then moisten with a spray bottle.

6. Place seed container(s) on a larger tray to catch drainage.

7. Cover loosely with a plastic lid or plastic wrap to maintain moisture. Make sure there is some airflow by keeping the lid ajar or making slits.

8. Select a sunny location such as a window to place tray(s).

9. Check daily to make sure the soil remains moist. If it looks dry, spritz with a spray bottle. Also look for any signs of mold. If found, scrape away and take off the plastic covering for more airflow to reduce the chance of mold returning.

10. When germination occurs and tiny seedlings begin pushing through the soil, take the lid off for good, to keep mold from developing.

Optional: Place tray(s) on a rubber heating mat to hasten germination.

Optional: If there is not adequate sunlight, consider purchasing grow lights. They should be suspended a few inches above the seedlings for best results.

 Benefits:

- Working with soil is another tactile activity, helping to acclimate those sensitive to touch, and allows sensory-seeking children the opportunity to have a touch-immersion experience.
- Planting tiny seeds requires fine dexterity, thereby building skill in this area.
- The placement of seeds utilizes spatial and visual discrimination.

Professional growers use seed cells, but if on a tight budget recycled food containers work well for starting seeds.

- Spray bottles are a super hand strengthener!
- There are many opportunities for cooperative group work.
- Daily monitoring or soil health and observation of seedling growth and health offers up a sense of responsibility and pride.
- Participants gain a greater understanding of how plants develop.

POTTING UP PRESENTS

Once seedlings grow to two inches, they need more room for the roots to spread out and suck in all the nutrients and water necessary to sustain growth. If left too long, crowding leads to stunted growth, and the plant will not thrive.

Chances are there are more seedlings than you have room for in your designated garden area. Potting up extra plants to give to friends, neighbors, and relatives can be a fun activity, especially when so many holidays occur in the spring (Spring Equinox, Passover, Easter, May Day, Cinco de Mayo, Memorial Day). Decorating pots prior to planting makes the gift extra festive.

Equipment:

- Organic potting soil
- Large waterproof bin
- Seedlings
- Water
- Plastic pots
- Spoon
- Plant sprayer

- Decorating materials (glue, paper, drawing materials)
- Newspaper to minimize mess and collect overflow soil
- Labels (craft popsicle sticks work) and permanent marker

Directions:

1. Dump potting soil into bin.
2. Gradually add water—keep stirring to make sure all the water is fully absorbed. Consistency of soil when done should be spongy.
3. If decorating pots, do this prior to planting. Sample ideas:
   a. Drawing then taping pictures to the pot
   b. Cutting out pictures to glue or tape on
   c. Decoupaging with torn colored tissue paper.
   d. Painting the pot themed colors (red, white, and blue for Memorial Day, pastels for Easter).
   e. Pasting a photograph for Mother's Day
4. Fill the pot $^1/_3$ full with soil.

5. Gently remove the seedling from cell, careful to handle only by the root bundle or leaves. Avoid holding by the tender stem. Tip for extracting from cell: slide thin plastic marker or knife around the inside edge to loosen the soil, then press or push up from the bottom.

6. If seedlings have grown together in one large flat, carefully lift out a section of soil and gently separate seedlings. Select the most robust to plant in a pot.

7. Place the seedlings in the pot with roots resting on the soil. Carefully spoon soil in to cover the roots and surround the seedling.

8. Gently pat the soil around the seedling to make sure it is firmly anchored in the soil. Water thoroughly if the soil is not completely moist.

9. Place pots on windowsill and water daily. Place the pot on something that will catch the water. Be sure to label each pot to identify the plant!

10. Tie a bow around the pot and it makes a lovely present for family and friends!

*The Cape Abilities group takes seedlings home
almost every week during the growing season.*

NURTURING NATURE

Benefits:

- Spooning the soil into pots is not difficult but requires some accuracy, thus tapping into fine motor and hand-eye coordination. It also requires focus and attention. However, with the newspaper to collect overflow, there is no problem for those who lack accuracy. It will just take a little longer to fill up the pot.
- Planting the seedling in the pot works best if one hand holds the seedling and the other spoons soil in around it. This requires bilateral motor coordination.
- Alternatively, one person can hold the plant while the other fills in the soil, making it a cooperative activity.
- The use of a plant sprayer is a hand strengthener.
- Decorating pots unleashes creativity.
  - The opportunity to watch the plant grow is rewarding.
  - Giving the gift of a plant is a joy and fills one with pride.

SWEET POTATO SLIPS (LATE WINTER/EARLY SPRING)

Each year I plan on growing sweet potatoes. The problem is sourcing the slips. Local nurseries don't carry them, and mail order companies require purchasing a minimum of twenty-five slips, much more than I have room for in my garden. Finally, I went online to figure out how to grow them myself. I discovered they are fun and easy to grow!

Equipment:

- Organic potting soil
- Recycled plastic container (big enough to fit the sweet potato)

- Organic sweet potato
- Water
- Recycled wide-mouthed bottle or tall glass
- Fish fertilizer (2-4-1): phosphorus is the main ingredient for root development
- Tomato/vegetable fertilizer (2-4-2)

FUN FACT

Playing in the dirt might make you smarter:

A study found that mice exposed to certain soil bacteria performed better in a maze than mice that didn't have the exposure.

Dirt = Cognitive Booster!

Directions:

1. Fill plastic container with potting soil (fill about halfway).
2. Add water. The consistency of the soil when done should be spongy.
3. Place organic sweet potato on top of soil. (Non-organic may have root suppressant and won't sprout.) Place in a warm, sunny location and keep moist.
4. Slips will grow from the surface of the sweet potato. When they are approximately six inches long, snip off at the base. If roots are already growing, try to pull them off the potato as well.
5. Place the slip in a container of water. In a few weeks, roots should grow.

NURTURING NATURE

6. If the slip already has grown robust roots, plant it in a pot.

7. Return slips to the warm, sunny location.

8. Add fish fertilizer to the water after roots begin to form.

9. When the outdoor temperature is consistently above 60 degrees and the soil temperature is 70 degrees or above, plant in the ground, at least 12–18 inches between each slip. Add fish fertilizer when planted.

10. Every 2 weeks, fertilize with the tomato/vegetable fertilizer (per instructions on the label).

11. Sweet potatoes have a long growing season. They die back in the fall. When the leaves yellow and brown, it's time to dig in and harvest!

12. Dig carefully, as the potatoes have tender skins. Using a trowel and your hands is the best!

13. Sweet potatoes need to cure for several weeks to reach their peak sweetness.

Growing sweet potatoes is easy and rewarding ... and a nutritious, delicious treat!

14. Gently brush off excess dirt and store in one layer in a cool, dry place with good airflow.

15. Sweet potatoes store very well in a cool location (55–60 degrees Fahrenheit) with some humidity, like a basement.

FUN FACT

Sweet potatoes are a super food! They reduce inflammation, boost immunity, protect eye health, improve digestion, and reduce the risk of cancer and other health issues. And they're delicious!

Benefits:

- Growing sweet potatoes provides an excellent visual example of this root vegetable's life cycle, from the formation of slips, to root growth, to harvesting in the fall.

- Digging up the harvest requires touching the dirt and tactile discrimination, visual discrimination, and the joy of unearthing such exceptional food!

TRANSPLANTING IN THE GARDEN (SPRING/SUMMER)

You've nurtured those tiny seedlings inside, watering and making sure they have plenty of sunshine. Before you know it, these fledgling plants will take off, roots filling every nook and cranny of their containers, while the stems and leaves strive for more sunlight. When the days get warm enough, take the plants to a shady location outside so they can acclimate gradually to an outdoor climate (cooler, windy, brighter).

After a week, the seedlings can graduate to dappled light before moving to full sunlight. This process is called *hardening off*, essentially training the plant to get tough enough to live and thrive outside.

If the plant requires warm temperatures, it needs to move back inside until it's consistently at or above 60 degrees at night. It's a temptation to rush this process, but a stressed-out plant is not happy and will get even with you later in the season (aka languish, get sick and die, or provide very little produce). Patience is a virtue and critical when raising plants.

Once the seedlings can tolerate full sun and the temperatures fall in the range listed on the seed packet, you can take them out to the garden, their new home. Be sure the garden beds have been fully prepped, including any amendments required for the soil. Have mulch ready to pack around the plants once they've been planted.

Equipment:

- Trowels
- Seedlings
- Fertilizer
- Mulch
- Knee pad
- Measure (a ruler or something that approximates the distance between each plant; for example, trowel length, width of fingers, pre-measured cardboard).

Directions:

1. Pre-measure and mark location for each plant.
2. Dig hole for each transplant.
3. Sprinkle a small amount of fertilizer into the hole.

4. Press sides of pot or cell to loosen the soil and roots.

5. Carefully push up from the bottom and extract the plant using two hands. (Do not pull from the stem—it will break.)

6. Make sure to untangle the root ball so all the root endings can suck up water and nutrients.

7. Place the plant into the prepared hole. (Make sure the hole is slightly larger than the root ball.)

8. Surround with soil. All of the roots should be covered, then press firmly.

9. Water thoroughly with a watering can or hose with a shower-head-type nozzle.

Special Tips:

- To remove seedlings from cells, take a plastic plant marker (or similar object like a small plastic knife) and slide it along the sides of the cells to loosen the roots. Wiggle a little, then tip the marker up from the bottom to ease the seedling out.
- After removing from the cell, gently pull the mass of roots apart so it appears to have two legs. Farmer Stephanie calls this "making pants" when she works with the kids in her school program.
- Planting on a calm, cloudy day is ideal. There is less stress (not too bright, hot, windy) as the plant adapts to its "new digs."

 ### *Benefits:*

- During the hardening-off period, cooperative work is required, taking turns transporting the plants to and from outside.

Providing a generous amount of mulch as soon as plants are in the ground makes them feel snug and comfy, keeps the soil moist, and saves work later in the summer, since the mulch suppresses weed growth.

- Watering is critical during the hardening-off period, which is a favorite, easy activity.
- Participants learn the proper technique for planting seedlings, including how to handle tender stems and the importance of proper adjustment of roots.
- Participants learn the importance of proper spacing of plants, learning that plants need space and ample opportunity for food and water, just like people.
- Participants learn/reinforce how to measure.
- There is an opportunity to tap into fine motor dexterity and bilateral motor control while working with the tender seedlings.
- There is an opportunity for touch input/tactile stimulation.
- Working with the soil exposes gardeners to beneficial microbes that are antibacterial and antiviral.

Chapter Five

SUNFLOWERS AND JOURNALING
(SUMMER & YEAR ROUND)

There's something spectacular about seeing a row of ten-foot-high sunflowers. Especially when you've personally planted the ¼-inch seed and watched it grow to become a towering behemoth. That's why the Truro Children's Community Garden grows sunflowers every year. Not only do the children watch them grow, but they measure the plants every week to track their growth in a journal.

There are many ways to *journal*. Along with measuring the sunflowers, at the end of each group, the kids assemble to eat fresh veggies harvested that day and document what has transpired during the group. They record the current weather conditions, including air and soil temperatures, tasks accomplished that day, and what they harvested. I am a lazy documentarian. After I make my garden plan and plant, I wait for the harvest. After weighing each haul, I write it down in a spiral notebook. At the end of the growing season, we add up the total number of pounds grown and estimate how much money we saved by growing rather than buying food at the grocery store.

Alternatively, group members can keep their own garden diary. It's an opportunity to document personal garden experiences, emotions, joys, and challenges.

Prompts can help facilitate reflections, such as follows:
- Sensations: What did you smell? What did you see? How did it feel?
- What was a challenge? Hard to do? Easy to do?
- What surprised you? What brought you joy?

- Did anything bring back a memory?
- What was your favorite thing today?

What to include in a journal is open-ended. You can document practical items related to planting:
- Planting and seed dates
- Bloom and fruiting dates
- Weather
- Soil amendments (compost, topdressing, mulching, fertilizers) and dates
- Harvest (what, weight)
- Troubles identified (diseases, pests, solutions to these problems)

And/or you can tap into creativity:
- Sketches and drawings of the garden, plants, etc.
- Photographs
- Quotes related to nature/gardening to share with the group
- Flowers that have been picked and placed between sheets of paper and pressed between two heavy books to preserve

Additional reference materials/information:
- Frost zone and planting schedules
- Seed packets (use plastic index card inserts in a 3-ring binder)
- Lists of companion plants (plants that like to grow together)
- Types of nutrients/food to give plants

Equipment:

- Any type of journal/notebook, fancy or plain. Or paper and a 3-ring binder
- Writing tools (pencils for easy corrections/erasing, pens, colored markers to augment creativity)

 Directions:

1. Keep journal(s) in a safe place and bring to the group. Distribute at each session.
2. Facilitate discussion. (Refer to prompts above.)
3. Consider adding creative activity (per suggestions above).

 Benefits:

- Reinforces learning concepts
- Opportunity to practice mindfulness (focusing on senses and immediate experiences)
- Reinforces writing and drawing skills
- Great group activity to foster discussion and sharing
- Helps with future garden planning and growing

PLANTING SEEDS DIRECTLY IN THE GARDEN (SPRING/SUMMER)

This is the moment you've been waiting for! You planned the garden, purchased the seeds, and prepared the garden beds. You checked the frost zone dates and confirmed the daily temperature for the next ten days. The hard work is already done, so gather the seeds, put on the garden gloves, and head outside. A trowel, knee pad, and marker to keep rows straight and tidy will help. Have a blast!

 Equipment:

- Trowels
- Measuring tool (ruler or something that approximates the distance between each seed (for example: trowel length, width of two fingers, piece of pre-measured cardboard)
- Seeds
- Fertilizer
- Marker to keep rows straight (for example, yardstick)
- Optional: knee pad (kneeling cushion)

Sunflowers

Chapter Five

Directions:

1. Pre-measure and mark location for each row. (Instructions are on the seed packet.)
2. Dig trench depth specified for seeds spaced close together.
3. Dig individual holes the depth specified and distance apart for plants requiring more space.
4. Sprinkle a small amount of fertilizer across the row or in the holes.
5. Place seeds in the trench/hole, cover and press firmly. Water thoroughly with a watering can or hose with a showerhead type nozzle.

Special Tips:

- For those who struggle with fine motor dexterity and/or visual acuity, select larger-sized seeds for them to plant, which are easier to see and manipulate.
- Alternatively, with small seeds, such as greens and carrots, you can broadcast the seeds: simply take a fistful and toss on a garden bed, then cover loosely with soil. Once the seeds germinate and grow approximately two inches tall, they can be thinned. Garden salads with baby greens are delicious!
- To create straight rows, use a guide such as the long handle of a shovel or other straight stick. Some kind of string can be laid down as long as there is a way to secure and keep it straight.

Benefits:

- Learning the proper technique for planting seeds
- Learning the importance of proper spacing of plants: learning that

plants need space and ample opportunity for food and water, just like people.

- Learning/reinforcing how to measure
- Tapping into fine motor dexterity when working with the tiny seeds
- Opportunities for touch input/tactile stimulation
- Exposure to beneficial microbes in the soil that are antibacterial and antiviral

COMPOST TEA (SUMMER)

While smelly, brownish-green liquid may not pique our appetite, plants love compost tea! Compost tea is a liquid organic fertilizer rich in vitamins, beneficial microorganisms, and antioxidants. Along with encouraging plant growth, the beneficial bacteria protect the plants from diseases. Making it is a simple process.

 Equipment:

- 2 five-gallon buckets
- Compost materials
- Non-chlorinated water (if chlorinated, leave in a pan twenty-four hours for chlorine to evaporate)
- Large strainer
- Large spoon, stick, or paddle for stirring
- Organic additives (coffee grounds, fish emulsion, seaweed/powdered, worm castings)
- Recycled bottles and funnel to store compost tea

Directions:

1. Fill a 5-gallon bucket about ⅓ full with finished compost material.

2. Fill the bucket with non-chlorinated water (well water, collected rainwater, and pond water are good sources).

3. Steep the tea concentrate for a minimum of 48 hours and up to a week. The longer it steeps, the stronger the mixture.

4. Stir daily, several times a day if possible. This aerates the potion, leading to increased beneficial microorganisms.

5. Strain into the second bucket using a fine mesh strainer. Rather than pouring the mixture, you may use a small pitcher or container, such as a quart-size yogurt container, to scoop out the mixture and pour it into the strainer.

6. Periodically, you may need to scrape out the solids from the strainer. Return the solids to the compost pile.

7. After all the strained liquid is transferred to the second bucket, save by filling recycled jugs or bottles with the mixture. Use a funnel for easy pouring and to avoid spillage.

8. Before applying to plants, dilute using a 10:1 ratio of water to tea.

9. Apply directly to roots, or use a plant sprayer and spray the leaves.

10. As a group activity, have members take turns scooping compost into a bucket, stirring daily, and then scooping liquid into a strainer.

Alternative: If available, seaweed makes an excellent tea, high in nutrients that plants love. If you live near the coast, an outing to collect seaweed is a great activity! Fill a bucket half way with seaweed, then fill with water, making sure the seaweed is completely immersed. The seaweed should steep for 2–3 weeks.

Optional: You can employ a more sophisticated process, which entails an electric aeration system, like an aquarium pump. Search online for information and resources if you have a hankering for the scientific/mechanical challenge.

Benefits:

- Each step is easy for anyone to perform (scooping, stirring).
- Great cooperative group activity!
- Plants love compost tea—it really bolsters the growth and health of the plant!

GOODY BAGS (YEAR-ROUND)

At the end of each Children's Garden group, the kids line up with a brown paper bag to gather treats from the day's harvest.

Equipment:

- Small paper bags (enough for each group member)
- Paper cups
- Paper towels
- Produce
- Markers

Directions:

1. Group members harvest whatever is growing in the garden (flowers, herbs, fruits, vegetables).
2. Hand out paper bags.

3. Group members put their names on their bags with markers.

4. Set up a table with the produce to bring home.

5. Line up, taking turns to select produce to bring home.

6. For cut flowers, wrap stem in wet paper towels and place in a paper cup.

 Benefits:

- Sharing the bounty with each other is a collaborative group experience.

- Members take pride in sharing produce that they helped grow with friends and family.

- Members get to eat delicious, healthy food.

SEED COLLECTING (LATE SUMMER/FALL)

When the garden begins to look drab and there's nothing more to harvest, many dying plants have one more gift to share: seeds. While vines whither and leaves turn brown, like a last gasp, some plants put all their remaining energy into creating seeds, thereby ensuring the continuation of future generations. So, before chopping, raking, and piling debris in the compost heap, harvest seeds for the next

Taste test: Which variety of tomato tastes best?

year's growing season. Some seeds are easy to spot and will easily fall off the stems. Others require surgical assistance.

In the fall, the Cape Abilities garden group slices cherry tomatoes and peppers to extract seeds. They pull dried beans from the pods and pluck cilantro, parsley, and dill seeds from stems. Once blossoms like sunflowers dry, they pry out whatever seeds the birds have left behind. When the group reconvenes the following spring, they plant the saved seeds in pots to take home. Another example of the cycle of life.

Equipment:

- Paper plates to collect seeds
- Paper towels or clean, dry cloth
- Seeds (from herbs, fruits, vegetables, and dried flowers)
- Markers and envelopes
- Plate or platter (depending on the number of seeds) for drying

Directions:

1. For seeds inside fruits (tomato, pepper, cucumber, squashes) cut open and extract the seeds. A butter knife or spoon might help, especially for those individuals hypersensitive to touch. The seeds will feel slimy. Otherwise, picking out with fingers will suffice.

2. After seeds are extracted, rinse thoroughly, making sure all the fruit matter is off.

3. Place rinsed seeds on a paper towel or clean cloth and pat to remove excess moisture.

4. Spread out on a plate or platter to air dry, making sure there's no

overlap. After a few days, toss to make sure all sides are dry.

5. When completely dry, place in envelopes with the date and type of seeds.

6. For dried seeds (beans, flowers, and herbs that have flowered then turned to seeds, like parsley, cilantro, dill, and chives), simply pull seeds out of the pods or off the stems. Gather loose seeds and place in labeled/dated envelopes.

Tomato seeds are gooey until dry: a good challenge for those hypersensitive to touch!

7. Seal and save for the next growing season.

Special Tips:

- It is good to stagger this activity over several weeks or months. Begin in late summer with the fruits like tomatoes and squash that are still growing. Herb and flower seeds can be harvested late into the fall after they have fully dried on the stem.

- If your crew really enjoys harvesting the seeds, in October, provide pumpkins to harvest seeds to eat. Prepare as above for storing.

- Alternatively, after pumpkin seeds are cleaned off, mix with olive oil, salt, pepper and any other spice you enjoy. Roast in the oven (see sample recipe below).

Benefits:

- Cooperative group work gathering seeds.
- Taps into fine motor dexterity and bilateral motor control working to extract seeds.
- Opportunity for tactile stimulation— learning to tolerate slimy sensation.
- Reinforces the entire cycle of growth.
- Cost savings, as you will not need to purchase as many seeds the next year.

Labeling envelopes for storing dried seeds is a great group activity.

Pumpkin Seed Recipe

1. Wash and dry seeds.
2. Toss with 1 tablespoon of olive oil.
3. Season with salt and pepper (may add paprika and garlic powder).
4. Roast at 350°F for 12–15 minutes, tossing every 5 minutes.
5. It is ready when seeds turn golden brown.

Pumpkin Seed Nutrition (A Super Food!)

Excellent source of fiber, zinc, iron, phosphorus, potassium, magnesium, and antioxidants like selenium and beta carotene.

(per ounce)	8.6 grams protein	3 grams carbohydrates
	14 grams healthy fats	1.7 grams fiber

Chapter Five

HARVESTING POTATOES (SUMMER/FALL)

Anyone who loves a treasure hunt or the idea of digging for gold will love harvesting potatoes! In the spring, toss chunks of organic potatoes onto a patch of fertile soil and cover it with compost and soil. When pretty green plants pop up, dump more soil around the plants. This is called 'hilling the potatoes," which allows more roots to grow. And growing more roots is the best, because these roots turn into potatoes!

Late summer and early fall, get down on your hands and knees, or squat and dig in. It is best to do this with your hands. Digging with a shovel may chop and injure the spuds. Besides, it's thrilling to dig and feel round lumps—aka potatoes. It feels like the earth is giving us a present, which it is!

Seed potato

 Equipment:

—To Plant—

- Trowel or shovel
- Measuring tool (ruler or something that approximates the distance between each plant, for example: trowel length, piece of pre-measured cardboard)
- Seed potatoes
- Fertilizer (higher percentage of phosphorous-to-nitrogen ratio, which facilitates root growth)

- Soil and compost
- *Optional:* knee pad
- *Optional:* Save the trouble of prepping bed and substitute a grow sack

—To Harvest—

- Trowel
- Basin or basket

- Tray, rack, or screen
- *Optional:* Gloves, knee pads

Directions:

—To Plant—

1. Prep garden bed.
2. Toss seed potato in bed: random or in carefully laid-out rows. They should be spaced 12–14 inches apart (all sides).
3. Dig holes 6 inches deep.
4. Sprinkle a small amount of fertilizer (approximately 2 tablespoons per hole).
5. Place seed in the hole. Make sure the cut side is down.
6. Cover with soil and compost. Press firmly. Water thoroughly with a watering can with a showerhead-type nozzle.
7. When plants grow approximately 8 inches high, bury half in soil/compost, leaving 4 inches of greenery. Repeat this after another 8 inches of growth.
8. When pretty flowers bloom, nip the buds so the energy gets redirected into more root development, rather than making seeds.
9. Make sure any potatoes that might poke through the ground get covered up. Light turns the exposed area green. Green sections of potatoes are toxic and should be cut out and *not* eaten.

—To Harvest—

1. When plants die back (you'll know—it's quite dramatic), the potatoes are ready to be dug up, but they can stay in the ground for a long time.

2. Use a trowel to break up the ground and loosen the soil, but it is best to dig with the hands to avoid breakage of the potatoes.

3. Dig directly below the dead plant. The potatoes can grow up to 18–24 inches deep, with some spreading out beyond the vine.

4. Expect to find potatoes of all different sizes.

5. Cure potatoes. This allows the skin to toughen up for better storage. Gently brush off dirt and place potatoes on a flat surface, ideally with airflow, like a cooling rack or screen. Place in a shady place with good airflow (for example, covered porch or garage).

Special tip: Digging up potatoes is labor intensive, so a good plan is to harvest discreet areas over time. Alternatively, if you have a big group, assign a specific area to each individual, based on their stamina and physical strength.

 Benefits:

- Harvesting potatoes requires heavy work (lifting, digging), which activates filters in the brain.
- It provides opportunities for touch input/tactile stimulation.
- Working with the soil exposes gardeners to beneficial microbes that are antibacterial and antiviral.
- Participants get the delightful reward of digging up food!

NURTURING NATURE

LASAGNA GARDENING (FALL)

When I hear the word *lasagna*, I think of mouthwatering noodles, oozing with melted cheese, tangy tomato sauce, and maybe some meat, infused with pops of garlic, oregano, and basil. Some would call lasagna the perfect meal, containing all the essential food groups: dairy, protein, grains, and veggies, all in one big savory bite.

That's exactly how your garden feels when you create a lasagna garden. After clearing the beds, rather than leaving the exposed soil to the elements, tuck the bed in with layers of materials that provide a big punch of nutrition while the garden overwinters. The process is simple, and your garden will love it!

Essentially, lasagna gardening is like a mini-compost heap on each bed, with a specific layering of browns (carbon) alternating with greens (potassium/phosphorus) and manures (nitrogen). Along with providing a balanced diet of nutrients, the layers protect the bed from invasive weed seeds and insects looking for a home to lay eggs, which wreak havoc when the tiny worms hatch and ravage young seedlings in the spring. Best of all, this feast creates a perfect environment for vermiculture. Worms love to eat cardboard, so they clamber there, helping to decompose and transform the piled-up material into rich, nutrient-dense soil.

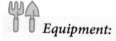 *Equipment:*

- Trowels
- Shovels
- Garden gloves
- Soil and compost
- Leaves, grass clippings, seaweed (the best!)
- Garden refuse (not diseased)
- Aged manure and/or compost
- Cardboard (best for worms!) Newspaper
- Coffee grounds and paper filters
- *Optional:* Straw (substitute for leaves) Peat

 Directions:

1. Weed and clear garden bed.
2. Gather all the ingredients (cardboard/newspaper, grass clippings, leaves (shredded best), garden refuse (chopped best), and manure/compost.
3. Layer the material in the following order:
   a. Place cardboard directly on the soil, completely covering the bed.
   b. Place 2–4 inches of chopped-up small twigs on top of cardboard for drainage.
   c. Dump on 8 inches of leaves or straw.
   d. Water the growing pile.
   e. Shovel on 2 inches of aged manure or finished compost.
   f. Place on top approximately 4 inches of grass clippings and other garden/yard waste. Coffee grounds can be included in this layer.
   g. Cover the entire mound with 8 inches of dried leaves or straw.
   h. Repeat the layers starting with #3.
   i. Water.

(While this is an ideal amount, your layers might not be as thick if you do not have enough material. Some addition is better than none.)

4. Let it sit all winter and cook away.

5. Keep the lasagna until you're almost ready to plant. The longer it sits, the more it "cooks."

6. Most likely some materials will not completely break down, so when ready to plant, lift what remains and put in the compost pile. Be careful to keep all those squiggly worms in the soil. They will keep busy aerating the soil, improving the structure by tunneling around and feeding the soil all their nutritious worm castings.

Benefits:

- This is a great cooperative group project—another example of "many hands make light work." Gathering and preparing the materials can be a multi-week process or one big work-a-thon kind of event.

- Everyone can participate. Shoveling, scooping, and tossing ingredients onto the pile—all these tasks require no special skills.

- This is a fabulous way to finish off the garden and prepare the beds to be super-healthy and productive in the coming year.

- This is a great way to get rid of grass, leaves, and other garden refuse in the fall! Why add to the overflowing toxic landfills when you can convert these materials into delicious soil for your garden?

Chapter Five

PUMPKIN RELAY (FALL)

The weather can turn cold on a dime in New England, limiting how much time the group can spend outside. Most of the kids are resilient and can tough it out in the colder temperatures, but some of the older adults in the Cape Abilities group have to be careful about their health and prefer not to participate when the temperatures dip below a certain point. A way to extend the garden season is to add some fun (okay, silly) games that can be played inside or out.

 Equipment:

- Pumpkins (size varies depending on the challenge you're looking for)
- Open large indoor or outdoor space
- Markers for the parameters of the course (anything: chair, bucket, pot)

 Directions:

1. Divide the group into two or three teams, depending on how many participants.
2. Mark the beginning and turnaround point.
3. Each team is given one pumpkin to carry up and back. Then they pass it off to the next in line. The first group that has all team members complete the loop wins.
4. Pumpkins can range in size and weight. Heavier pumpkins provide more challenge.

Variation: For kids with boundless energy, substitute crab walking for walking. Crab walking requires hard bodywork; it is a great workout and activates filters in the brain. This process is calming and helps facilitate better focus and attention.

Benefits:

- Team building and fun socialization
- Opportunity for fun!

VEGETABLE TAG (ALL YEAR)

Gardening shouldn't be all work and no play. At the Truro Children's Community Garden, after all the chores are done, the kids frequently play a game that entails running. While adults may find gardening a rewarding but laborious process, kids find it energizing. What better way to channel that energy then coupling the excess with concepts they've learned. Just weeded the beet bed? The go-to vegetable to shout out is BEETS!

Equipment:

- Open space to move around
- Prompts (if necessary): list or pictures of vegetables

Directions:

1. Someone volunteers (or is selected) to be "**it**."
2. Group members run around, trying to avoid getting tagged. If they are being chased and are about to get caught, they can sit down and

yell out the name of a vegetable. This is the equivalent of reaching base, where you're safe and can't be tagged.

3. If someone gets tagged before saying the name of a vegetable, they become **it**.

Adaptation: If sitting down is physically difficult, instruct participants to stand still while yelling out a vegetable.

Benefits:

- Requires recall of fruit/vegetable names.
- Reinforces learning from the gardening session.
- Motor planning challenge: running and remembering to name a vegetable simultaneously.
- Opportunity to exercise.
- Great social activity.
- It's fun!

BUTTERFLIES (YEAR-ROUND)

One could say that butterflies are one of the greatest wonders of the world. A lowly caterpillar emerges from an egg, crawls around munching on leaves and whatnot until sated, and then finds a place to hang (literally) by a silk thread it makes. One or two weeks later a beautiful butterfly emerges from the chrysalis. These majestic beauties not only add color to the garden, but they contribute to the pollination of many plants.

Butterflies are fascinating to watch. As they sip a flower's nectar, they hardly move, making it easy to view the intricate patterning and vibrant colors of their wings. Suddenly they take flight, whirling up, sometimes floating skyward, often to alight on another flower nearby. The stillness and bursts of movement are a visual delight.

In all of Truro's garden programs, the kids learn about the butterfly's life cycle, their importance in nature, and people's role in providing food. The Truro Children's Community Garden has planted milkweed, the only food monarch butterfly larva (the caterpillars) can eat. The Cape Abilities group enjoys feeling the fluffy milkweed seeds, but mostly they love watching the butterflies flit around the garden.

Some people create gardens specifically to entice butterflies to come visit, choosing plants that butterflies find attractive and tasty. But anyone can create an environment welcoming to butterflies. Tucking in a few marigolds, nasturtium, and calendula, all beneficial companions to vegetable plants, will attract a host of these winged beauties. By adding flowering herbs such as dill and parsley, you'll turn your garden into a butterfly magnet!

Equipment:

- Flowering plants in bright colors that attract butterflies (red, orange, yellow, pink, and purple blossoms)
- Native flowering plants
- Flat-topped clustered flowers
- Milkweed

Chapter Five

Butterflies appeared 200 million years ago, before flowering plants!

A group of butterflies is called a *flutter*.

Butterflies feed on plants' nectar with a tube-like tongue called a *proboscis*.

Butterflies taste with their feet and smell with their antennae. Their eyes detect motion and color and can see forward, backward, above, and below all at the same time, along with seeing ultra-violet light, which humans can't see. Some species can hear, and some make clicking sounds to communicate.

 Directions:

1. Plant vegetation that attracts butterflies. Make sure the plants are in sunny locations. Butterflies can only fly when the air temperature is between 60 and 108 degrees Fahrenheit. They like sunshine and are known to bask in the sunlight, spreading their wings to get warm enough to fly.

2. Observe the butterflies in the garden. To extend the activity, provide paper and colored pencils/markers to draw the butterflies.

3. To make a deep-dive butterfly study, you can purchase kits to watch the full cycle of butterfly life:
   - Larva (caterpillar)
   - Pupa (chrysalis) 10–15 days
   - Butterfly (adult)

🏆 *Benefits:*

- While observing butterflies is a passive activity, it is a shared group experience.
- This is a visual wonder. Observing nature has a relaxing effect on people.
- This activity provides the opportunity to learn about ecology and the interdependence of nature and humans.
- Encouraging the propagation of butterflies is good for the garden and the world.

Can you find the monarch butterfly?

Chapter Five

The Amazing Story of Monarch Butterflies

Toward the end of winter, monarch butterflies (MBFs) in Mexico and Southern California mate. The male dies, and the females head north, feeding on nectar along the way. They deposit eggs on milkweed plants, which is the only food the larva will eat when they hatch from the egg.

Eventually the butterflies die, but the eggs they deposited along their route turn into caterpillars, which feed on milkweed leaves. For two weeks they eat constantly and grow by shedding their skin. Then they search for a place to attach themselves to a leaf or branch and transform into a pupa (chrysalis). After attaching, they shed their skin and form a hard shell. After nine to fifteen days, fully formed butterflies emerge.

The entire egg-to-butterfly process is called *metamorphosis* and takes about a month. The new MBFs continue north, feeding on nectar of milkweed, clover and goldenrod. As the days cool, they head south in search of warmer weather. The trip takes about two months, and they travel three thousand miles! The average life span of MBFs is six to eight months. They have been placed on the Endangered Species List. The population has had an alarming decline due to development that eliminates milkweed, and pesticides that kill these magnificent insects.

GARLIC PLANTING (FALL)

Myths about garlic repelling vampires might not be true, but it's super-power for combating disease and promoting health is. Garlic is a superfood and is super delicious. It's also easy to grow and fills in the gaps of the growing season perfectly. After you've harvested all the food and cleared out and prepped the beds for winter, it's time to bring out the shovel one last time to plant the garlic.

 *Equipment:*

—To Plant—

- Trowel
- Measuring tool (a ruler or something that approximates the distance between each garlic clove)
- Garlic seed (individual cloves of garlic)
- Fertilizer (5-10-10, nitrogen-phosphorus-potassium: aka tomato/vegetable)
- Soil and compost
- Mulch

—To Harvest—

- Trowel
- Basin or basket
- Tray, rack, or screen
- Optional: gloves, knee pads

Chapter Five

Directions:

—To Plant—

1. Prep garden bed.
2. Choose healthy, large garlic cloves (the bigger the clove, the bigger the garlic bulb when harvested). Break cloves from bulb a few days before planting. Keep the husk on each clove.
3. Immediately before planting, work the fertilizer into the soil, several inches below where the base of the garlic clove will rest (approximately 4 inches deep).
4. Plant cloves 4–8 inches apart and 2 inches deep. Place the root side in the soil and the pointed side facing up.
5. Rows should be 6–12 inches apart.
6. Cover with soil and compost. Press firmly. Water thoroughly with a watering can or hose with showerhead-type nozzle.
7. Mulch.
8. In early spring, side-dress with compost and fertilizer. Repeat in late spring and again as the foliage begins to yellow.
9. Nip off any flowering, so the energy goes to the root, not making seeds.
10. Weed regularly. Garlic does not like competition!
11. Water regularly (every 3–5 days), but taper off just before harvesting, usually mid-June.

—To Harvest—

1. When plants die back (the leaves brown and wilt), garlic is ready to be dug up. This usually occurs early in the summer, but depends on the location and weather. Garlic is usually ready at the end of spring crop harvesting (like spinach, snow peas, radish) and before summer crops come in (tomatoes, peppers, eggplant, squash). Before harvesting everything, pull up a few to determine readiness. The bulb should have a thick, dry, paper-like covering. If the wrapping is thin, it's too early.

2. Use a trowel or garden fork to break up the ground and loosen the soil. Carefully dig up the bulbs. Do not remove the foliage or roots.

3. Cure garlic: this allows the skin to toughen up for better storage. Gently brush off dirt and place on a flat surface, ideally with airflow, like a cooling rack or screen. Place in a shady, dry place with good airflow (for example: covered porch or garage) for approximately 2 weeks. Alternatively, hang garlic upside down in bunches of 4–6 bulbs. When the wrappers are dry and papery and the roots are dry, the garlic bulbs can be stored. Brush off remaining dirt, trim roots to 1/4 inch, and cut tops to 1–2 inches.

4. Storage: Bulbs should be stored at approximately 55 degrees in a dark, dry place. A refrigerator is too cold and humid.

Benefits:

- Participants get opportunities for touch input/tactile stimulation.
- Working with the soil exposes gardeners to beneficial microbes that are antibacterial and antiviral.

- Garlic begins growing early in the spring. It is exciting to see a crop emerge when mostly nothing else has popped in the garden.
- Participants get the delightful reward of digging up food.

☀ FUN FACT

Garlic has been used for seasoning food and as a health agent for thousands of years. Garlic cloves were discovered in King Tut's tomb!

Health Benefits of Garlic

- Improve cardiac health
- Reduce risk of blood clotting
- Fights bacterial diseases, viruses, fungi, and parasites
- Reduce the risk of some cancers

With good airflow, when garlic cures, it can be stored for many months.

CHAPTER SIX

Special Populations Considerations

While the activities outlined in the previous chapters provide tips for making garden activities accessible to all, certain groups are confronted with specific challenges. This chapter will dig into concerns for those with physical limitations and the visually impaired. Specific strategies are reviewed along with equipment and supplies tailored to these needs.

 ## Physically Challenged

Those that are wheelchair bound or using walkers face challenges that able-bodied individuals don't have to reckon with. Likewise, individuals with poor motor coordination, balance issues, the frail, and those with low endurance might find it difficult to navigate and fully participate in garden activities. With careful planning, gardens can be created so that the beds are easily accessible and safe. Garden tools and equipment can be modified. The following is a step-by step guide for going about this:

I. ACCESSIBILITY

- Pathways around the garden need to be wide enough for wheelchairs and walkers to access and maneuver easily: 5-feet wide is ideal, while 4-feet wide is the absolute minimum.
- Pathways should be on level ground and free of obstacles. The surface should be hard and smooth. Woodchips and grass walkways are not advisable due to uneven surfaces and potential ruts and are difficult to propel through. Pavers and bricks are better if tightly laid out, but over time gaps and uneven stones can occur, making maneuvering difficult. Hard, smooth surfaces are best. Refer to the box with recommended surface options to make gardens more accessible.
- If major changes to the pathways are not an option, consider a mobility mat that leads to the raised beds designated for the physically challenged.
- Raised beds make it possible for people using wheelchairs and walkers to access the garden. Raised beds should be high enough to minimize reaching and bending. A height of 24–30-inches is ideal. If the bed has access on all sides, then the width can be up to 4 feet. If the bed is against a fence or wall, then the bed should only be 2-feet wide; otherwise, reaching and working in the bed becomes difficult.

- Elevated table beds are another, excellent option. As they have open space underneath, wheelchairs can scoot under, making it even easier to work. Likewise, worktables for planting seeds, transplanting, etc. should allow clearance for wheelchairs.
- Consider using pots and planters. Planters can be placed higher using plant stands.
- Consider planting vertical gardens with trellises. Refer to box for suggested plants that thrive when grown vertically.
- Some planters are specially made with wheels, so the planter can be moved for easier access. Alternatively, planters can be placed on small dollies that can move.

Two examples of accessible garden beds. Note the black landscape fabric, which is an affordable ground covering, making movement with a wheelchair or walker easier.

II. SPECIALIZED TOOLS

Garden tools can be specialized to make them easier to reach and grasp. Built-up handles with foam wrapped around are an easy solution for comfort and ease in holding tools. Healthcare product companies have developed specific handles that are easier to grasp without injury to wrists. This is especially helpful for those with arthritis or immature grasping patterns and poor fine motor control.

Here is a list of adaptive tools and strategies that make gardening less physically demanding and more successful:

- Foam padding for easier gripping
- Gloves with a sticky surface to minimize slippage
- Ergonomic garden tools: specifically designed to protect joint integrity and easier manipulation
- Extended-reach hoes and cultivars
- Reachers/grabbers to retrieve things beyond arm's reach
- Plant equipment caddies to carry supplies
- Lightweight tools

The Cape Abilities participants take great pride in the small herb garden they've planted and nurtured throughout the season.

Chapter Six

III. MOBILITY OPTIONS

For those who are not wheelchair bound, but find mobility precarious, or have low endurance, there are several options to facilitate working in the garden. Some are stationary, and others allow the gardener to scoot around without the need to stand up.

- Knee pads work well for individuals who are confident moving around and want to kneel down on the ground to work but find squatting too fatiguing. Kneeling on the pad provides comfort and reduces stress.
- Garden seats are great for individuals who can walk around but are more comfortable sitting while working on a garden bed. These are lightweight and easily moved to other locations in the garden.
- Rolling garden carts are an all-in-one option. They feature a seat on top of a cart used to haul supplies.
- Garden scooters, in which a seat is attached to heavy-duty wheels, so the gardener can scoot around.

Options for Pathway Surfaces

Heavy-duty landscape fabric can be rolled out after the ground has been thoroughly leveled and packed down. Be sure to tack down edges securely.

- Crushed stone: ¼ minus grade gravel with pieces ¼ inch or smaller and angular shapes allows the particles to lock together. Once packed down, it creates a cement-like surface. Correct installation requires excavating at least six inches, first adding a layer of coarse gravel for adequate drainage. Regular maintenance is required, as ruts, erosion, etc., can occur.

- Stabilized decomposed granite: This involves mixing loose granular material with a stabilizing agent. When sprayed with water and allowed to dry, the stabilizer binds the granite particles together, creating a solid, durable surface, which is resistant to erosion, cracking, and shifting.

- Asphalt and concrete are the most expensive options and require equipment and skilled workers to install. But after the initial outlay of labor and cost, they are the easiest to maintain, most durable, and most effective surface for maneuvering with a wheeled vehicle.

Plants That Thrive in a Vertical Garden

Pole beans	Strawberries
Cucumbers	Morning glories
Peas	Clematis
Summer squashes	Climbing rose
Eggplants (varieties that are narrow like Asian)	Climbing hydrangea
	Verbena and lantana
Tomatoes	Nasturtium

Chapter Six

Visually Impaired

Gardens conjure up images of beautiful colors and patterns soothing to the eyes, essentially, a visual feast. While less obvious, other senses are tweaked as well. Gardens offer an array of sensations that can soothe, excite, and bring pleasure, especially for the visually impaired. In chapter 3, each of the senses is reviewed, and plants that complement these senses are listed. For instance, the rustling leaves of a fig tree and the sweet fragrance of peonies provide great pleasure, sight unseen. The velvety soft texture of lamb's ear and the tactile discovery of fruit ready to harvest can bring joy to all, notably for the visually impaired, who rely on other senses to engage in the world.

Similar to the constraints for those with physical limitations, safety and easy access to the garden are paramount. Methods of planting can alleviate difficulties and minimize frustration. With careful planning, gardening can be as pleasurable, if not an even greater source of joy, for the visually impaired.

This strawberry is just asking to be discovered and plucked.

NURTURING NATURE

I. ACCESSIBILITY

- Easy access to and around the garden is key to safety and success. Pathways should be level and free of obstacles. They do not need to be wide, but there should be consistency in the width. 3 feet is a comfortable width.
- While some surface variability is possible, pavers, bricks, grass, and woodchips can have divots, washouts, and uneven surfaces, making movement around the garden treacherous. Refer to the box with recommended surface options.
- Once the layout and walkways have been established, strolling through the garden several times a day for a week or so will provide a level of familiarity and comfort prior to the added challenge of gardening chores.
- Narrow raised beds (2–4 feet wide), planters, and vertical gardens make it easier to reach and work with vegetation.

II. GETTING ORGANIZED

- Garden equipment should be stored in an accessible and organized way. Braille labels can be used on containers, bins, and shelving to easily identify tools, etc.
- Garden caddies with compartments streamline tool usage in the garden.
- Create a landscape/garden map to identify the location of beds.
- Label pots and beds with signage to identify plants.
- For a sensory garden, plan to locate plants with distinct aromas together in bunches or clusters, and separate other fragranced

plants in another area. That way, olfactory cues will help identify locations in the garden. For example, clusters of basil can grow near companion plants such as tomatoes. Separate other fragrances such lavender in another location in the garden. Consider plants that have distinct sounds for added enjoyment. (Refer to the "Sensory Benefits" chapter).

III. WEEDING STRATEGIES

- Plant in blocks, clumps, or rows to easily identify the chosen plant from weeds.
- Mulch heavily to suppress weeds around the plants.
- For individuals with low vision, tie bright-colored ribbon on plants. When there is no vision, create a barrier such as tomato cages, or cutout plastic containers to surround the base of plant.
- Help participants become familiar with the feel of seedlings and the maturing plant through tactile exploration. Likewise, help them identify through touch, the shape and texture of unwanted growth (e.g. weeds).

Placing protectors around plants helps to identify location of plants by touch.

IV. SOWING SEEDS

- Sprinkle seeds into a container with sides so the seeds don't scatter. Make sure it's large enough for fingers to reach in and pinch a small number of seeds. Teach participant to rub with thumb and index finger until holding just one seed.
- Modular seed tray method: Teach the participant to work systematically from one side of the tray to another. Use plastic markers to identify each row.
- Seed tape: A nice alternative is to purchase pre-spaced seeds. Tape with seeds attached can be planted in troughs, or directly into planters and beds.
- Direct seeds into garden beds. Place a marker such as a yardstick, to maintain straight rows. Use a premeasured object to maintain accurate spacing. (For example, trowel scoops are often 5-6 inches long.)

V. PLANT MAINTENANCE

- Ease of watering: consider irrigation systems. Alternatively, retractable hoses minimize the danger of tripping and tangling. Lightweight hoses that don't kink are key. Watering cans should have showerhead nozzles so the spray disperses over a wider area.
- Pruning requires tactile exploration and familiarity with the plant. Teach participants to feel upward from the base of the plant to identify the main stem, differentiated from side shoots.
- Harvesting: Many plants and flowers provide tactile cues: size, shape, and texture. For example, the leaves of an onion plant flop

over and dry up. It is easy to feel the size of cucumbers, squash, beans, and greens to determine ripeness. Tomatoes are trickier and require a taste test, or visual assistance from a friend.

VI. PROTECTION FROM WASPS

Bees and wasps are important workers in the garden. They're critical for pollination and often prey on invasive (bad) insects. Honeybees are mild mannered. Even if you accidentally brush against them, they tend to just move on rather than retaliating with a sting. Wasps on the other hand, are aggressive, stealthy predators. They are territorial and don't want to share the space they are working on. When I see a wasp nearby, I move to a new area of the garden. This obviously poses a problem for the visually impaired. So one strategy is to entice wasps to a location away from an area to be cultivated. Here are a few strategies:

- Wasps *love* sugar in all forms. They especially like sugary liquids (like fruit juices and soda) and fruit. Place these enticing goodies far from the area to be worked, but still in the vicinity of the garden. The wasps will hopefully decide they'd much rather have a Dr. Pepper than work hard to access the nectar in a squash blossom.
- Wasps *do not* like the smell of certain plants, specifically marigolds, geraniums, mint, and basil. If you tuck these into garden beds, they might deter wasps from foraging there and keep to the fragrances they prefer.
- Wasps are repelled by peppermint oil. Make a mixture of peppermint essential oil and water. Spray in the vicinity to be worked and maybe even apply to skin and clothing.

CHAPTER
SEVEN

The Evidence:
Why We Garden from a
Scientific Perspective

We have reviewed the many ways that nature and gardening contribute to everyone's well-being. Specific activities outlined many benefits for health, personal growth, socialization and cognitive development. Studies sprinkled throughout the book underscored the importance of engagement in the natural world. This chapter will go into more detail regarding some of the previous studies cited and introduce others to expand and deepen your understanding of these scientific underpinnings.

The studies highlighting the benefits of nature are overwhelming, so you may ask: if just walking outside helps so much, why go to all the trouble of gardening? Or you may wonder if immersion in nature translates to gardening. Apparently it does. The second half of the chapter will focus on studies that specifically look at the beneficial outcomes of gardening as well as horticulture programs targeting special populations.

The Healthy Impact of Viewing Nature

Health care providers have noticed that patients who have a view of the outdoors seem to recover faster. Florence Nightingale, the famed nurse in the nineteenth century, remarked on the improvements in patients when they could see the open sky. Countless anecdotal reports since then have identified views of tress and landscapes as beneficial to recovery.

Psychologist and architect Roger Ulrich came up with the hypothesis that nature views could reduce stress and lead to improved clinical outcomes, so he devised a study comparing hospital outcomes for patients with and without a nice view. He examined the records of gallbladder surgery patients for many years at one hospital in Pennsylvania. Ulrich identified those who had rooms with a view of trees and the unlucky patients who had a window looking at a brick wall. The patients looking at trees had fewer postoperative days in the hospital, requested less pain medication, and had better attitudes as reported in nurses' notes. The study was published in *Science* magazine in 1984 and got a lot of attention. As a result, many health care practitioners have included nature scenes in their office décor!

Roger Ulrich was a busy man. After the hospital study, he wanted to figure out why people have improved health outcomes when they look at nature. He ran several studies, using electroencephalograph devices (EEG), which measure brain activity. In the first study, one group of volunteers looked at slides of nature while the second group saw scenes of utilitarian urban buildings. The nature group showed higher alpha wave activity (a wavelength associated with relaxation, meditation) and increased serotonin (the feel-good chemical).

The subjects in a different study were not so lucky. Before viewing nature versus non-nature scenes, Ulrich stressed out all participants by making them watch gory videos of bloody accidents. He confirmed that they were stressed-out by measuring sympathetic nervous system (SNS) activity: increased sweating, heart rate, and blood pressure. The SNS is activated when we're anxious, terrified, angry and/or fearful, not feel-good states.

After the stress-out session, one group was assigned to a ten-minute video of nature scenes, and the other group watched urban scenes. Within five minutes, the nature group returned to baseline (calm states). The participants in the urbanscape group remained stressed out, and still hadn't fully recovered even after ten minutes.

Rachel and Stephen Kaplan have been studying the effects of nature on our brain's ability to rest and recover since the '80s. They developed a hypothesis: Attention Restoration Theory (ART), which essentially boils down to our need to take a break from higher-level cognitive thinking (top-down). Whether trying to solve complex equations, coordinate the daily to-do list, or navigate a traffic jam, our brains have to work hard. ART posits that the brain fatigues from all this hard thinking. Attention, efficiency, and proficiency wane. However, when we take a break

FUN FACT

In the past decade or so, with amazing technological advances, scientists can look inside our brains and have begun to unravel what's going on.

- The EEG (electroencephalograph units) can analyze brain waves like alpha (relaxation), beta active (thinking/alertness), and gamma (sensory processing) in real time.
- Blood flow studies show where the brain is working hardest. Just as muscles require oxygen to work, the brain sops up more oxygen in active areas. So blood rushes to areas of high activity.

Study after study demonstrates the positive effects of nature on brain activity.

and walk in nature, the top-down brain thinking slows down and the bottom-up, or unfocused, processing of sensory information takes over, thereby giving the brain a break. This allows the higher cortical centers time to re-boot or become restored. Many of the scientists trying to unravel the mysteries of nature's effect on the brain have embraced the concepts formulated by the Kaplans.

Flash forward a few years, and technology offered up a new invention: mobile EEGs. Let's call them EEG caps, which are essentially mobile EEG devices that read brain wave activity away from the lab. Scientists were finally able to take a look at what the brain does while walking in the forest, in the park, or on a hectic city street. They no longer had to rely on pictures. They could immerse subjects in the real world!

David Strayer, another neuroscientist studying the psychological and cognitive effects of outdoors, thinks nature is a powerful antidote to the constant distraction of our digital lives. He believes nature enhances higher-order thinking, restores attention, and boosts creativity. With a cohort of colleagues, he ran studies looking at people walking in urban and natural settings wearing the EEG cap.

The findings are complicated and difficult to understand if you haven't studied neuroscience. Essentially, they found that higher-order thinking—like multi-tasking—uses a lot of brain power, but when walking in natural settings, the brain quiets down. In the study's conclusion, they state the following:

> This study demonstrates that prolonged time in nature relates to fluctuations in neural biomarkers. ... Immersion experiences in nature may alter neural signatures that relate to a tendency to focus on internal thoughts and increase awareness of the external environment. ... Nature influences neuroelectrical power during rest.

To decode this a bit, "internal thoughts" refers to ruminations, like worrying thoughts looping through our heads, often associated with anxiety and depression. Awareness of the external environment relates to that constant vigilance we employ to stay connected, muddling through our day and focusing on the necessary tasks at hand. The "fluctuations" while in nature refers to the decrease in top-down thinking, thus allowing us to take a break, regroup, and be able to focus better after getting recharged.

Nature as Medicine

Living near the ocean, I can attest to the calming effect of water views. As soon as I cross the dune and look at the expanse of water, my thinking literally shifts. The ruminations that occupy my half-mile walk disintegrate, and I become absorbed in the moment: gulls overhead, blustery wind in my face, smell of low tide. My mind wanders, and often in those unfocused moments, the phrase or passage I struggled to write will pop into my head. The dog sits patiently by my side as I type this *discovery* into my phone. I know when I return to my desk, all the "top-down" cortical thinking will flood my brain and I'll struggle to retrieve my *epiphany*.

Chapter Seven

Sometimes I choose a longer walking loop. Wending through a small pine grove by the side of the road, whether on my way to or from the beach, I feel a deeper calm settle over me, unlike the settled feeling I experience at the bay. I once attributed this feeling to happy memories of hiking in the woods earlier in my life. Now I know that the pine trees are bewitching me.

Evergreens emit chemicals in the form of aerosols. We are familiar with the fresh smell of pine, especially when we bring a fresh-cut Christmas tree into the house. Manufacturers capitalized on the positive effects by incorporating the aroma into cleaning products, such as Pine Sol, reminding us how fresh and clean our home will be if we scrub it down with their product.

NURTURING NATURE

Aromatic tree smells come from *phytoncides* (essential oils like terpenes, pinenes, limonenes), but we just call it a fresh pine smell. Scientists suspected that these aromatic essential oils emitted by evergreens and other trees may be increasing our ability to fight diseases along with reducing stress. Sure enough, their studies are discovering exactly that: phytoncides (note the *-cide* in the word—like insecticide) increase the production of *killer cells* in our bodies: white blood cells that our immune system produces to fight diseases. But we're getting ahead of ourselves. Let's start with a walk in the woods.

An activity trending recently is called *forest bathing*. People walk into the woods, or maybe a city park with lots of trees. A guide trained

Walk in the Woods vs. Urban Walk

Yoshifumi Miyazaki, a physical anthropologist, and his colleague, Ju-young Lee, went about proving that by engaging all five senses while walking in nature, we become fully alive, and there are healthful physiologic benefits. To prove that our physiology responds to different habitats, they have taken hundreds of research subjects into the woods and compared these leisurely forest strolls with urban walks. They found the following for those on the nature walks:

- 12 percent decrease in cortisol levels (the stress hormone)
- 7 percent decrease in SNS activity (fright-flight-fight response)
- 1.4 percent decrease in blood pressure
- 6 percent decrease in heart rate
- Self-reports of better mood and decreased anxiety

in meditation has the participants focus on trees, incorporating breathing and meditation. The objective is to achieve a state of mindfulness in nature. While relatively new to the United States, it is hugely popular in Japan. With almost 92 percent of Japan's population living in densely populated urban settings, it makes sense that people are wrangling to find effective ways to get back in touch with nature. And it makes sense that scientists in Japan are looking at this closely.

Intrigued by all the data coming out verifying our body's healthy response to nature, Quing Li, an immunologist, decided to investigate. He wanted to figure out what was going on with our immune system and decided to study cells that float around in our blood stream looking for enemies to destroy. The actual name of the cells he studied is *natural killer cells* or *NK cells* for short!

NK cells are a type of white blood cell that protects us from disease agents by sending self-destruct messages to tumors and virus-infected cells. (Does this sound like *Mission: Impossible*?) Stress, aging and pesticides have been found to reduce your NK count, which is a bad thing. It means you are less able to fight illnesses. The good news is that it is possible to increase your NK cell count. Li figured out how.

NK cells are easily measured in the lab. Li decided to test if nature's ability to reduce stress might increase NK cell production, thereby enhancing our ability to fight diseases. In his first experiment, he took a group of businessmen into the woods for three days. They hiked a few hours each day. At the end of their adventure, their killer cells had increased 40 percent! That boost lasted seven days. A month later the NK count was still 15 percent higher than prior to their excursion.

Another (not so lucky) group were stuck tromping around an urban setting for the same duration with equivalent physical exertion. They had no change in their killer cell level. Li has run many more experiments with people representing various demographics (for example, women), and each time came up with similar results. Time in the forest leads to significant increases in immune-boosting NK cells.

A cynical reader may be thinking, "Great, but who has time to disappear in the woods for three days?" Happily, Li studied one-hour trips into city parks and found similar results. The NK count increased, just not as much as during a three-day immersion experience.

So what's going on with these aerosols? Li suspected that the aromatic essential oils emitted by evergreens and other trees may be increasing NK production. After such success sequestering businessmen in the wilderness for three days, he decided to gather a group of thirteen subjects and lock them inside hotel rooms for three nights. Some of the rooms had humidifiers pumping out essential oils from cypress trees while they slept. Other rooms had humidified air with just vaporized water. Those inhaling the cypress-infused air experienced a 20 percent increase in their NK cells after three nights. That group also reported feeling less fatigued. The control group (those without added aromatic vapors) had no change in their NK cell count.

Li refers to cypress oil as a miracle drug. Excited by these results, he returned to his laboratory and paired NK cells with phytoncides (like the cypress oil) in a petri dish. Then he watched the NK cells multiply. A few other players joined the petri dish party. In addition to natural killer cell increases, other anticancer agents that cause tumor cells to self-destruct proliferated.

So struck by his findings, Li says he uses a humidifier with cypress oil almost every night in the winter. He also suggests choosing natural environments when planning a vacation, visiting parks on a regular basis, and *gardening*!

The Curative Nature of Gardening

So let's direct our attention to gardening. Gardening is not a walk in the woods or forest bathing, where you can inhale those healthful phytoncides—that is, unless you plant a garden near a forest or stand of trees. Gardening requires digging in the soil, which unearths more surprising findings: Scientists have looked at the composition of soil and discovered health-enhancing features in the *dirt*!

In Li's studies, he looked closely at phytoncides, the aromatic tree smells that include terpenes. These are fancy names for chemical molecules. We might not understand the chemical formulations but we know a terpene when we smell it!

Close your eyes, and think of a hot, dry summer day. The sky becomes overcast and the air heavy. You become aware of an earthy scent and know that it's about to rain. That's because you're smelling geosmin, a terpene that is manufactured by soil organisms. Geosmin is found everywhere in the world, especially in the soil. The most prolific producer of geosmin is streptomyces bacteria. This four-syllable word sounds familiar because it has been used by the pharmaceutical industry for years.

Mark Buttner is a microbiologist who has studied geosmin and thinks there's a symbiotic relationship, hypothesizing that geosmin enhances the propagation or ongoing production and spread of streptomyces bacteria. This is a big deal. Buttner says, "Streptomyces is one of the most important sources of antibiotics known to science."

While there are still several hypotheses floating around regarding the role geosmin plays in the production of this bacteria, we do know that where there's geosmin, streptomyces bacteria will be nearby, the very organism that the pharmaceutical industry has made billions of dollars selling, and health care providers have relied on for decades to keep us healthy. So when you dig into the soil, your skin is likely exposed to geosmin and streptomyces, this life-saving medicine.

While some scientists were busy in labs and locking people up in hotel rooms to discover the health benefits of nature, others focused specifically on gardening. In 2011, Agnes Van Den Berg, Mariette Custers, and associates investigated the impact of gardening. Like Ulrich with his nature versus urban picture study, they stressed-out thirty study participants. Rather than showing them gory pictures like Ulrich did, the subjects had to take a difficult test to make them anxious. Then half the subjects were sent out to garden and the other half stayed inside to read. Cortisol levels (that stress hormone) and self-reported mood were measured before and after. Cortisol levels in both groups decreased, but the decline was much greater in the gardening group. Mood was fully restored in those who gardened, but further deterioration was reported in the folks who read inside. These findings indicate that gardening promotes relief from stress.

Having a Household Garden Makes People Happy

Large-scale studies have demonstrated that gardening makes people feel happy. A group of urban planners looked at the emotional well-being of participants living in the city who had small household gardens. They found that household gardening was associated with high emotional well-being. Interestingly, vegetable gardening, as compared with other types of landscape gardening, resulted in the most satisfaction. They also found that gardening alone at home was as pleasurable as working with a group.

Jenny Roe and colleagues have been studying the effects of gardening in a myriad of ways in the UK. One fascinating study looks at elderly adults who continue to thrive well into their eighties. These researchers wanted to determine what factors led to such vibrant lives in spite of aging bodies. They found that natural settings, including personal and public gardens, are the single most important place in terms of offering psychological restoration and recovery from fatigue and stress.

Gardening is a passion in the UK, so it's not surprising that scientists wanted to figure out why folks love it so much. L. S. Chalmin-Pui and colleagues ran a study to look specifically at the benefits of gardening. In their article: "Why Garden? Attitudes and Perceived Health Benefits of Home Gardening," the key takeaways were the following:

- Increased frequency of gardening correlated with health benefits.
- Gardening at least two to three times a week maximized health benefits.
- Pleasure, not health, was the stated prime motivation to garden.
- People with existing health issues particularly acknowledged the value of gardening.
- Satisfaction and engagement improved as the amount of green space increased in the garden. (Bigger is better!)

Chapter Seven

The Therapeutic Value of Gardening

The evidence continues to grow: exposure to nature and gardening leads to improved health, a sense of well-being and enjoyment. But does this translate to special populations, who beat to a different drummer, so to speak? Many studies focus on gardening programs for vulnerable populations. Let's begin with studies looking at the impact of horticulture therapy programs geared toward neurodiverse populations.

Horticulture therapy integrates social and behavioral science with horticulture and the environment. Horticulture therapists use garden activities as the medium for targeting specific therapeutic goals, such as increasing socialization. Several recent studies highlight beneficial gains for individuals with autism spectrum disorder (ASD) when engaged in a horticulture therapy program.

Two professors in the College of Agriculture in Kerala, India, W. S. Nevil and G. K. Beela, looked at the impact of a horticulture therapy program on ten participants with ASD. They employed the case study research method to look at unique aspects of each individual. They were interested in seeing if participating for one month in a horticulture therapy program would lead to an increase in social intelligence. Six out of the ten participants fully participated. Using a standardized test, these individuals had increased their social intelligence. The four who participated inconsistently and did not fully engage when present demonstrated no improvement in their social intelligence score and corresponding behavior. The researchers note that in spite of the short

intervention time period, the gains made by those who fully participated support the stated goals of the study:

- Greater verbal/gestural communication and interpersonal interactions
- Increased initiation and completion of tasks with greater independence
- Improved adaptive behaviors

Emotional Intelligence

An area that people with ASD often struggle with is emotional intelligence (EI). EI is the ability to manage your own emotions and
understand the emotions of people around you. Five key elements of EI
are as follows:

- Self-awareness   • Empathy
- Self-regulation   • Social skills
- Motivation

Beela teamed up with another colleague to study the impact of a
statewide horticulture therapy program on the emotional intelligence
of children with ASD. Forty-four kids ranging in age from ten to fifteen
years old participated in a one-year program. The study demonstrated
that horticulture therapy improved the emotional intelligence of these
students.

Neurodiverse individuals often experience stress and anxiety as
they struggle to self-regulate and figure out how to navigate in a world
filled with neuro-typical individuals, many of whom are sadly not

terribly empathic of their plight. The studies highlighted earlier in this chapter provide mounting evidence of how natural settings and gardening reduce stress as well as provide added health benefits.

Fighting Dementia

Victims of Alzheimer's disease are some of the most vulnerable in our society. The number of individuals diagnosed with this disease continues to grow. As research grapples with this growing health crisis, attention has turned to strategies beyond pharmaceuticals in the hopes of finding therapeutic programs that will extend and enhance the quality of life for those diagnosed with this devastating disease. One method with growing support is horticulture therapy.

Before diving into studies reviewing the positive effects of gardening for those with dementia, let's take a quick look at the history of horticulture therapy. While considered a relatively new player in modern medical rehabilitation, the use of horticulture to calm the senses goes back to 2,000 BC in Mesopotamia. Gardens throughout the ages have provided solace for the bereaved and overwrought.

☁ SAD FACT

Based on a 2023 report compiled by the Alzheimer's Association, an estimated 6.7 million Americans sixty-five years of age and older are living with Alzheimer's disease.

NURTURING NATURE

In the nineteenth century, Dr. Benjamin Rush, considered the Father of American Psychiatry, identified the curative benefits of garden settings for the mentally ill. He writes, "Digging in a garden was one of the activities that distinguished male patients who recovered from their mania from those that did not engage in garden activities." A professor of the Institute of Medical and Clinical Practices at the University of Pennsylvania, he made sure the hospital grounds had tree-lined paths through grassy meadows. Since then, many private and public hospitals have included agriculture and gardening activities in their programs.

Horticulture therapy further expanded during World War I. Up to this time, occupational therapy and recreational therapy used gardening in psychiatric settings. As wounded veterans flooded US hospitals, the use of horticulture therapy expanded to medical settings. The Rusk Institute of Rehabilitative Medicine, associated with New York University Medical Center, was the first to add a greenhouse to

Benefits of Horticulture Therapy

Studies in horticulture therapy have demonstrated many benefits:
- Improved sleep, agitation, and cognition in dementia patients
- Acquisition of new skills and regaining of lost skills
- Improved memory and attention
- Increased social interaction
- Reduced stress
- A sense of accomplishment and increased self-esteem
- Reduced pain perception

its Rehabilitation Unit. By the 1970s a separate horticulture therapy curriculum was created at Kansas State University. Since then, formal educational programs have proliferated, and horticulture therapy has become a well-respected profession.

Recent studies have looked at the value of therapeutic gardens for dementia patients. Wander gardens are therapeutic gardens specifically designed for safety and geared toward residents with dementia. Here are some of the special considerations of these gardens:

- They are enclosed to prevent elopement.
- They provide easy access to the residential facility.
- Their pathways are cleared of obstructions to minimize the risk of falling.
- Their plants are edible and no pesticides are used.

Having the freedom to stroll around an inviting outdoor space seemed like a good idea to Mark Detweiler, who wondered if a wander garden might improve the behaviors of the residents at a residential facility. He developed a study with associates, looking at specific quantifiable behaviors. Thirty-four male residents were observed for twelve months before a wander garden was opened, and then for the next twelve months when the wander garden became available at their facility. Behaviors were systematically measured, including incident reports of disruptive behaviors, extra medications needed, and surveys of staff and family members regarding their interactions with the residents.

After the wander garden was available for twelve months, results showed that the number of incident reports for agitation and anxiety was reduced. There was also less need for extra medication to combat agitation. Staff and family members also reported that the wander garden decreased inappropriate behavior and improved mood and the quality of the men's lives.

Understanding the importance of remaining physically active, Detweiler and associates also examined whether a wander garden could have an impact on the residents' ability to walk and mitigate falling risks. The results are dramatic. The study participants experienced a decrease of approximately 30 percent in the number of falls and the severity of injuries resulting from falls after the garden opened. Those who visited the garden the most saw falls decrease almost 39 percent, while those who used the garden infrequently only had about an 8 percent decline in falls.

Fear of falling is not only a concern for those struggling with dementia. Growing older puts stress on many systems for all those reaching their golden years. The loss of brain cells occurs as we age, and this loss accelerates the older we get. Scientists have found that stress exacerbates this decline. Prolonged episodes of stress and anxiety increase cortisol levels, which lead to changes in the brain. These changes lead to decreased cognition and function. As function declines, the ability to live independently becomes more difficult.

The sixty-five years and older age group is experiencing its fastest growth rate in a century. Care facilities, from assistive living to total care, are a financial burden for individuals and their families. There is a huge cost to the public sector. Finding ways to extend the vibrant independence of individuals becomes more urgent as these numbers soar.

Chapter Seven

FUN FACT

According to the US 2020 census, one in six people in the United Sates are sixty-five and older.

In 2023, the Alzheimer's Society reported that taking regular, physical exercise appears to be one of the best things to stave off dementia. Studies have shown that regular exercise in mid-life reduces the risk of developing Alzheimer's by 45 percent. A literature review of many studies looking at brain function over sixty-years of age found a clear link between physical activity levels and cognitive performance, suggesting that exercise might be an effective way to reduce cognitive decline later in life. Optimal physical activity recommended is twenty to thirty minutes of aerobic exercise regularly. Examples of this kind of exercise include brisk walking and gardening.

This book is a guide to gardening, not a compendium of research to support the premise that nature and gardening are critical to our health and well-being. We have skimmed the surface of all the studies reinforcing this assertion. Other studies have looked at the positive influence on the self-esteem of physically challenged populations. A myriad of research continues to flow in regarding the power of stress reduction through gardening and nature.

Neurodiverse populations struggle with stress and self-esteem. The elderly wrestle with deteriorating abilities and the associative need to adjust, often accompanied by stress, anxiety, and depression. Isolation and lack of opportunities to go outdoors and absorb all those healthful benefits frequently occur for many of these vulnerable groups.

Hopefully, the evidence regarding the critical importance of regular trips outside and the many benefits of gardening will be compelling enough that individuals, families of a child with special needs, practitioners in educational programs, caretaking facilities, and therapeutic settings will determine that nature and gardening need to be a priority!

I began gardening to have a few moments of peace and maintain my sanity. My boisterous toddlers have grown into full-fledged adults with lives of their own. I clamor to grasp any time they'll give me. I regale them with fresh greens and whatever else is growing at the time of their visits as I relay the latest antics from our gaggle of hens. When they leave, I send them off with their own vegetable goody bags. To fill the void after their departure, I turn to my garden, which has grown from one small box to dozens of raised beds. I find solace in the visual beauty, the sweet aromas, and the bounty wrought from the small swath of land I've managed to cultivate and nurture and, in turn, nurtures me.

Chapter Seven

Entrance to the author's garden. Wilbur the pig greets all the visitors.

I met Maddie Ahrensefeld many years ago, when we worked on sensory processing and motor development. Maddie hated holding a pencil! With perseverance and an indomitable spirit, she overcame many hurdles and developed a passion for drawing. Living on a small farm, once her sensory system regulated, she was able to immerse herself in nature, accessing the many benefits plants and animals offer. Maddie and I crossed paths again when we both moved to Cape Cod. She'd grown into a self-confident and talented artist, creating whimsical artwork featuring nature and reminding us that joy can be found in the natural world. When Maddie learned that I had a new book coming out, she created this design, reimagining vegetables and flowers growing in the garden. Her creations, M.A. Designs can be found at Reciprocity, Harwich, Massachusetts, Maggie Ruley~Island Inspirations, Key West, Florida and online: http://www.reciprocityharwichport.square.site

NOTES

CHAPTER 2

"Vitamin D is produced" ... "Vitamin D Fact Sheet for Health Professionals," National Institutes of Health Office of Dietary Supplements, *NIH*, September 18, 2023, https://ods.od.nih.gov/factsheets/VitaminD-HealthProfessional/#: – :text=Together.

"Along with bone and muscle help" ... "Vitamin D," The Nutrition Source, Harvard T. H. Chan School of Public Health, March, 202, https://www.hsph.harvard.edu/nutritionsource/vitamin-d/.

"FUN FACT In the winter" ... "Vitamin D," The Nutrition Source, *Harvard T. H. Chan School of Public Health*, March, 2023, https://www.hsph.harvard.edu/nutritionsource/vitamin-d/.

"absence of sunlight leads to myopia" ... Florence Williams. 2017. *The Nature Fix*. New York: W. W. Norton & Company. p. 6.

"efficiency of using two hands" ... Jill Mays. 2011. *Your Child's Motor Development Story*. Arlington, Texas: Sensory World. pp. 97-100.

"Motor Planning" ... Jill Mays. 2011. *Your Child's Motor Development Story*. Arlington, Texas: Sensory World. pp. 145-146.

CHAPTER 3

"Examples of Textured Vegetation" ... Kendra Wilson. 2022. *Garden for the Senses*. New York: DK Publishing. pp. 40-48.

"These proprioceptors send" ... Jill Mays. 2011. *Your Child's Motor Development Story*. Arlington, Texas: Sensory World. p. 16.

"SAD FACT People who produce" ... Florence Williams. 2017. *The Nature Fix*, New York: W. W. Norton & Company. p.25.

"FUN FACT The brain is made up" ... George Markowski, "Physiology," Britannica.com, (Science and Mathematics) accessed December 20, 2023, https://www.britannica.com/science/information-theory/Physiology.

"Many studies have documented" ... Florence Williams. 2017. *The Nature Fix*, New York: W. W. Norton & Company, 2017. pp. 89-91.

"FUN FACT Bird song" ... Richard Sima, "Why Birds and Their Songs Are Good for Our Mental Health," *Washington Post*, 5/18/23. Based on the following studies:

E. Stobbe, J. Sundermann, L. Ascone, and S. Kuhn, "Birdsongs Alleviate Anxiety and Paranoia in Healthy Participants," *Scientific Reports*, 12, no. 16414, 2022, https://www.nature.com/articles/s41598-022-20841-0?itid=lk_inline_enhanced-template.

R. Hammoud, S. Tognin, L. Burgeess, N. Bergou, M. Smythe, J. Gibbons, N. Davidson, A. Afifi, I. Bakolis, & A. Mechelli, "Smartphone-Based Ecological Momentary Assessment Reveals Mental Health Benefits of Birdlife," *Scientific Reports*, 12, no. 17589, 2022, https://www.nature.com/articles/s41598-022-20207-6?itid=lk_inline_enhanced-template.

"Plants for listening pleasure" and *"FUN FACT Plants react to sound"* ... Kendra Wilson. 2022. *Garden for the Senses*, New York: DK Publishing. p. 152.

"Natural plant extracts" ... "Aromatherapy: Do Essential Oils Really Work?" HopkinsMedicine.org, Johns Hopkins Medicine Health, online, accessed December 20, 2023, https://www.hopkinsmedicine.org/health/wellness-and-prevention/aromatherapy-do-essential-oils-really-work.

"FUN FACT Lemon Balm" ... "Lemon Balm," Mt. Sinai Health Library, Mt. Sinai Today Blog, last modified January, 2024, https://www.mountsinai.org/health-library/herb/lemon-balm#:.

"Plants for Olfactory Pleasure" ... Some listed in Kendra Wilson. 2022. *Garden for the Senses*. New York: DK Publishing. pp. 100-108.

"Fractals are geometric shapes" ... "What Is a Fractal?" Internal. Accessed December 20, 2023, https://iternal.us/what-is-a-fractal/#: – :text=A%20Fractal%20is%20a%20type.

"In 2008 humans officially became an 'urban species'" ... Florence Williams. 2017. *The Nature Fix*, New York: W. W. Norton & Company. p. 11.

"The visual cortex" ... Florence Williams. 2017. *The Nature Fix*, New York: W. W. Norton & Company. p.116.

"FUN FACT The magic of viewing" ... Florence Williams. 2017. *The Nature Fix*, New York: W. W. Norton & Company. pp. 175-176.

"FUN FACT Potted plant study" ... M. Detweiler, T. Sharma, J. G. Detweiller, P. F. Murphy, S. Lane, J. Carman, A. S. Chudhary, M. H. Halling & K. Y. Kim, "What Is the Evidence to Support the Use of Therapeutic Gardens for the Elderly?" *Psychiatry Investigation*, vol. 9, no. 2, June, 2012, pp. 100-110.

CHAPTER 4

"USDA" ... "USDA Plant Hardiness Zone Map," US Department of Agriculture, online, accessed January, 10, 2024, https://planthardiness.ars.usda.gov/.

Notes

CHAPTER 5

"FUN FACT Mycobacterium vaccae is a bacterium" ... Bonnie L. Grant "Antideressant Microbes In Soil: How Dirt Makes You Happy" *Gardening Know How* online, February 27,2023, https://www.gardeningknowhow.com/garden-how-to/soil-fertilizers/antidepressant-microbes-soil.htm#:~:text=Did%20you%20know%20that%20there's,makes%20you%20relaxed%20and%20happier.

"FUN FACT Blood flow study" ... Florence Williams. 2017. The Nature Fix, New York: W. W. Norton & Company. p. 69.

"Compost Recipes and information about" ... Deborah L. Martin, Barbara Pleasant, *The Complete Compost Gardening Guide*. 2008. North Adams, MA: Storey Publishing.

"FUN FACT According to the EPA, municipal solid waste" ... "National Overview: Facts and Figures on Materials, Wastes and Recycling," Environmental Protection Agency (EPA), online, November, 2023, https://www.epa.gov/facts-and-figures-about-materials-waste-and-recycling/national-overview-facts-and-figures-materials.

"Worm Farms" ... Adrian White, "How to Start a Worm Farm at Home: Learn About Vermiculture," *Gardener's Path*, online, April 29, 2023, https://gardenerspath.com/how-to/composting/worm-farming-vermiculture/.

"FUN FACT Earthworms have assisted" ... J. Tharakan, A. Addagada, D. Tomlinson & A. Shafagati, Department of Chemical Engineering, Howard University, Washington, DC, USA.

Waste Management and the Environment II, V. Popov, H. Itoh, C.A. Brebbia & S. Kungolos (Editors) © 2004, WIT Press, www.witpress.com, ISBN 1-85312-738-8, https://www.witpress.com/Secure/elibrary/papers/WM04/WM04012FU.pdf.

"FUN FACT Playing in dirt makes you smarter" ... Ker Than, "Depressed? Go Play in the Dirt," *Live Science*, April 11, 2007, https://www.livescience.com/7270-depressed-play-dirt.html.

"FUN FACT Sweet potatoes are a superfood" ... Megan Ware, "What's to Know about Sweet Potatoes," *Medical News* Today, online, 6/26/2023, https://www.medicalnewstoday.com/articles/281438.

"Pumpkin Seed Recipe" ... Jessica Gavin, "How to Roast Pumpkin Seeds," Jessica Gavin, *Culinary Scientist*, online, 2/26/2022, https://www.jessicagavin.com/how-to-roast-pumpkin-seeds/.

"Pumpkin Seed Nutrition" ... Mary Jane Brown, "Top 11 Science-Based Health Benefits of Pumpkin Seeds, *Healthline*, online, January 11, 2023, https://www.healthline.com/nutrition/11-benefits-of-pumpkin-seeds#TOC_TITLE_HDR_2.

"Lasagna Gardening. Directions" ... Jenny Blackwell, "Make a Lasagna Garden in a Raised Bed," *Brooklyn Botanical Garden*, bbg.org, September 23, 2016, https://www.bbg.org/article/make_a_lasagna_garden_in_a_raised_bed.

"FUN FACT Butterflies appeared" ... "Butterflies," Wikipedia, online, last modified January 10, 2024, https://en.wikipedia.org/wiki/Butterfly#: – :text= .

"The Amazing Story of Monarch" ... "Monarch Butterfly," *National Geographic Kids*, accessed February 6, 2024, https://kids.nationalgeographic.com/animals/invertebrates/facts/monarch-butterfly.

Catherine Boeckmann, "How to Plant, Grow, and Harvest Garlic," *Almanac Growing Guides*, online, accessed, December 4, 2023, https://www.almanac.com/plant/garlic.

"FUN FACT Garlic has been used" ... "Garlic: Is It Good For You?" Web MD Editorial Contributors, Web MD, online, accessed December 20, 2023, https://www.webmd.com/diet/garlic-good-for-you.

CHAPTER 6
"Sowing seeds for blind" ... The Geoffrey Udall Centre, "Gardening When Blind or Visually Impaired," Thrive, Reading, UK, online, accessed January 10, 2023, https://www.thrive.org.uk/get-gardening/gardening-when-blind-or-visually-impaired#.

CHAPTER 7
"Roger Ulrich came up with the hypothesis that nature views" ... Roger Ulrich, "View Through a Window May Influence Recovery," *Science*, vol.224, no. 4647, 1984, pp.224-25 ... in The Nature Fix p. 108-7.

"Ulrich stressed out" ... Roger Ulrich, "Stress Recovery During Exposure to Natural and Urban Environments," *Journal of Environmental Psychology*, vol. 11, pp 201-30. ... in *The Nature Fix* p. 27.

"Rachel and Stephen Kaplan and Attention Restoration Theory" ... Florence Williams. 2017. *The Nature Fix*, New York: W. W. Norton & Company. p. 49.

"Attention Restoration Theory" ... "Nature as a Potential Modulator of the Error-Related Negativity," *International Journal of Psychophysiology*, Vol. 156, October, 2020, pp. 49-59.

"David Strayer, another neuroscientist" ... Carolyn Gregoire, "The New Science of the Creative Brain on Nature," *Outside Magazine*, online, 5/12/2022, https://www.outsideonline.com/health/training-performance/new-science-creative-brain-nature/.

Notes

"This study demonstrates" ... David Strayer, et. al. "Nature as Potential Modulator of Error-Related Negativity," *International Journal of Psychophysiology*, vol.156, October, 2020, pp.49-59.

"92 percent of Japan's population" ... Aaron O'Neill, *Statista*, 8/17/2023, https://www.statista.com/statistics/270086/urbanization-in-japan/#: –.

"Walk in the Woods vs. Urban Walk" ... Yoshifumi Miyazaki ... Florence Williams. 2017. *The Nature Fix*, New York: W. W. Norton & Company. p. 23.

"Quing Li, an immunologist ... studies natural killer immune cells" ... Qing Li et. al., "Effects of Phytoncide from Trees on Human Natural Killer Cell Function," *International Journal of Immunopathology and Pharmacology*, vol. 22, no. 4, 2009. pp. 951-959 ... in The Nature Fix pp 28-29.

"Microbiologist Buttner has studied geosmin" ... Alex Fox, "How Rain Evolved Its Distinct Scent and Why Humans Love It," *Smithsonian Magazine*, online, April 17, 2020, https://www.smithsonianmag.com/smart-news/smell-rain-explained-180974692/.

"Agnes Van Den Berg ... investigated the impact of gardening" ... A.E. Van den Berg and M. H. Custers, "Gardening Promotes Neuroendocrine and Affective Restoration from Stress," *Journal of Health Psychology*, vol. 16, no.1, 2011, pp. 3-11.

"Having a Household Garden Makes People Happy" ... Graham Ambrose, Kirti Das, Yingling Fan, Anu Ramaswami, "Is Gardening Associated with Greater Happiness of Urban Residents?" Landscape and Urban Planning, *Elsevier* 100072, January 31,2020, https://www.sciencedirect.com/science/article/pii/S0169204619307297?ref=pdf_download&fr=RR-2&rr=84473dd19f6a05e0.

"Studying the effects of gardening" ... Jenny Roe, Mark Blythe, Caroline Oliver, Alice Roe, "Flourishing 'older-old' (80+) Adults: Personal Projects and Their Enabling Places," *Well-being, Space and Society*, Vol.3, 2022, 100072, https://www.sciencedirect.com/science/article/pii/S266655812200001X?ref=cra_js_challenge&fr=RR-1.

"L.S. Cahlmin-Pui ... look at benefits of gardening" ... Lauriane Suyin Chalmin-Pui, Alistair Griffiths, Jenny Roe, Timothy Heaton, Ross Cameron, "Why Garden? Attitudes and Perceived Health Benefits of Home Gardening," *Elsevier* Vol. 112, May 2021, 103118, https://www.sciencedirect.com/science/article/pii/S0264275121000160.

"Two professors ... looked at the impact of horticulture therapy" ... Nevi, W. S. and Beela, G. K., "Impact of horticulture therapy in social intelligence of people with autism spectrum," *International Journal of Autism Disorder*, January 2023, https://scholar.google.com/ scholar?q =Impact+of+horticulture+therapy+in+social+intelligence+of+people+with+autism+ spectrum&hl=en&as_sdt=0&as_vis=1&oi=scholart.

"Emotional Intelligence" ... Mental Health America National, online, accessed January 10, 2024, https://mhanational.org/what-emotional-intelligence-and-how-does-it-apply-workplace.

"Beela ... impact of a statewide horticulture therapy program on the emotional intelligence" ... G. K. Beela, H. Thankappan, "Horticulture Therapy Program in Kerala Improves Emotional Intelligence of School-Going Children with Autism Spectrum Disorder," *International Society of Horticulture Science*, Nov. 2021, https://www.ishs.org/ishs-article/1330_2.

"SAD FACT Based on a 2023 report" ... Alzheimer Association, "2023 Alzheimer's Disease Facts and Figures," *Alzheimer's Dementia*, 19, no. 4, 2023, DOI 10.1002/alz. https://www.alz.org/alzheimers-dementia/facts-figures#: – :text= .

"History of horticulture therapy" ... M. Detweiler, T. Sharma, J. G. Detweiller, P. F. Murphy, S. Lane, J. Carman, A. S. Chudhary, M. H. Halling & K. Y. Kim, "What Is the Evidence to Support the Use of Therapeutic Gardens for the Elderly?" *Psychiatry Investigation*, vol. 9, no. 2, June, 2012, pp. 100-110, https://www.ncbi.nlm.nih.gov/pmc/articles/PMC3372556/.

"Benefits of Horticulture Therapy" ... Mark B. Detweiler, Taral Sharma, et. al., "What Is the Evidence to Support the Use of Therapeutic Gardens for the Elderly?" *Psychiatry Investigations*, no. 2, June 9, 2012, pp.100-110, https://www.ncbi.nlm.nih.gov/pmc/articles/PMC3372556/.

"Having the freedom to stroll" ... Mark B. Detweiler, Taral Sharma, et. al., "What Is the Evidence to Support the Use of Therapeutic Gardens for the Elderly?" *Psychiatry Investigations*, no. 2, June 9, 2012, 100-110. https://www.ncbi.nlm.nih.gov/pmc/articles/PMC3372556/.

"Scientist have found that stress exacerbates decline" ... "Exercise as Medicine to Prevent Cognitive Decline," Public Health Center of Excellence, Alzheimer's Association, 2023, https://www.alz.org/media/Documents/exercise-ph.pdf.

"FUN FACT According to the US 2020 census" ... "2023 Alzheimer's Disease Facts and Figures," *Alzheimer's Dementia*, 19, 4, 2023, https://www.alz.org/alzheimers-dementia/facts-figures.

"In 2023, the Alzheimer's Society report" ... "Physical Activity and the Risk of Dementia," Alzheimer's Society, 2023, https://www.alzheimers.org.uk/about-dementia/managing-the-risk-of-dementia/reduce-your-risk-of-dementia/physical-activity.

"Other studies have looked at the positive influence on self-esteem of physically challenged" ... Beela G. K. Reghunath B. R., "Horticulture Therapy on Self Esteem and Motor Skills of Physically Challenged Children," *Indian Journal of Physiotherapy and Occupational Therapy—An International Journal*, April 2021, https://www.researchgate.net/publication/350941318_Horticultural_therapy_on_self_esteem_and_motor_skills_of_physically_challenged_children.

RESOURCES

FDA FROST ZONES

"USDA Plant Hardiness Zone Map," US Department of Agriculture, accessed January 19, 2024, https://planthardiness.ars.usda.gov/.

"2024 First and Last Frost Dates," Almanac Online, updated January 12,2024, https://www.almanac.com/gardening/frostdates.

SOIL TESTING

"Soil Testing Is Worth the Effort," *Fine Gardening*. By: Lee Reich (Issue 108), accessed January 25, 2024, https://www.finegardening.com/article/soil-testing-is-worth-the-effort.

"College Partner's Directory" USDA National Institute of Food and Agriculture, accessed January 19, 2024, https://www.nifa.usda.gov/land-grant-colleges-and-universities-partner-website-directory.

GARDEN PLANNING

Arricca Elin SanSone and Christopher Michel, "21 Garden Layout Ideas for Every Size Garden." *Country Living*, September 22, 2023, https://www.countryliving.com/gardening/garden-ideas/g746/garden-plans/. *(This article covers many specific types of gardens, including pollinator garden, kitchen gardens, fragrant garden herb garden, raised planter patio garden, and vertical garden.)*

Catherine Boeckmann, "20 Vegetable Garden Layout Ideas (with plans!)," Almanac Online, December 28, 2023, https://www.almanac.com/over-20-vegetable-garden-layout-ideas. *(This article outlines how to lay out many kinds of gardens, including square-foot gardens, backyard gardens, raised beds, kitchen gardens, homestead gardens, small gardens, companion gardens, drought-resistant gardens, and partial shade gardens.)*

Ame Vanorio, "10 Functional and Productive Vegetable Garden Plans," Insteading, 11/2/2020, https://insteading.com/blog/vegetable-garden-plans/. *(This article includes an Urban Homestead vegetable garden, Cook's Choice vegetable garden, 3 Season Raised Bed Vegetable Garden, Wood Pallet Garden, and a variety of sized gardens with suggested layout.)*

Tara Nolan, "4 x 8 Raised Bed Vegetable Garden Layout Ideas," Savvy Gardening, accessed January 5, 2024, https://savvygardening.com/4x8-raised-bed-vegetable-garden-layout/. *(This article provides more tips for raising vegetables in limited spaces and how to maximize the yield.)*

"Grow and Give: Grow Food and Share the Harvest," Colorado State University Extension, accessed January 5, 2024, https://growgive.extension.colostate.edu/garden-plans/. *(Several garden plans are provided, including a Community Garden Plot plan, First Timers' Garden plan, Succession Planting Garden plan, and Easy Peasy High-Yield Garden plan.)*

NURTURING NATURE

SMALL GARDEN INFORMATION
Kevin Espiritu. 2021. *Grow Bag Gardening: The Revolutionary Way to Grow Bountiful Vegetables, Herbs, Fruits, and Flowers in Lightweight, Eco-friendly Fabric Pots*. London: Cool Springs Press.

Tammy Wylie. *Raised-Bed Gardening for Beginners: Everything You Need to Know to Start and Sustain a Thriving Garden*. 2019. New York: Callisto Media.

Joel Karsten, "What Is Straw Bale Gardening?" Straw Bale Gardens Online, accessed January 9, 2024, https://strawbalegardens.com/.

COMPOST RESOURCES
Barbara Pleasant, Deborah L. Martin. 2008. *The Complete Compost Gardening Guide*. Belmont, California, Wadsworth Publishing Company.

"Composting at Home," EPA United States Environmental Protection Agency Online, accessed January 19, 2024, https://www.epa.gov/recycle/composting-home. *(This website offers comprehensive information regarding composting, answering all the whats, hows, whys, and more.)*

Adrian White, "How to Start a Worm Farm at Home: Learn about Vermiculture," Gardener's Path Online, (4/29/2023) https://gardenerspath.com/how-to/composting/worm-farming-vermiculture/.

SEED SAVING
International Seed Saving Institute www.seedsave.org.

SEED CATALOGS AND ONLINE SOURCES
Almanac, "Free Garden Seed and Free Plant Catalogs," (1/10/2024) https://www.almanac.com/content/garden-seed-catalogs-mail.

The author has used:
Johnny's Selected Seeds
    https://www.johnnyseeds.com/catalog-request/

Fedco Seeds
    https://fedcoseeds.com/

High Mowing Seeds
    https://www.highmowingseeds.com/

Territorial Seeds
    https://territorialseed.com/

Resources

HORTICULTURE THERAPY

Rebecca Haller, Karen Kennedy, Christine Capra, eds. 2019. *The Profession and Practice of Horticulture Therapy*. Boca Raton Press, FL: CRC Press.

Rebecca Haller, Christine Capra, eds. 2016. *Horticulture Therapy Methods: Connecting People and Plants in Health Care, Human Services, and Therapeutic Programs*. Boca Raton Press, FL: CRC Press.

AROMA THERAPY

Valerie Ann Worwood. 2016. *The Complete Book of Essential Oils and Aromatherapy, Revised and Expanded: Over 800 Natural, Nontoxic, and Fragrant Recipes ...* Novato, California: New World Library.

Susanne Fischer-Rizzi, Illustrators: Peter Ebenhoch, Gunter Hartmann. 1991. *Complete Aroma Therapy Handbook: Essential Oils for Radiant Health*. New York: Sterling Publishing Company.

ACCESSIBLE GARDENING

Adil, Janeen. 1994. *Accessible Gardening for People with Disabilities: A Guide to Methods, Tools and Plants*. Bethesda, MD: Woodbine House.

Rothert, Gene. 1994. *The Enabling Garden, Creating Barrier-Free Gardens*. Dallas: Taylor Publishing Company.

Woy, Joann. 1997. *Accessible Gardening, Tips and Techniques for Seniors and Disabled*. Mechanicsburg, PA: Stackpole Books.

Yeomans, Kathleen. 1992. *The Able Gardener, Overcoming Barriers of Age and Physical Limitations*. Pownal, VT: Storey Communications Inc.

Pollock, Annie and Marshall, Mary. 2012. *Designing Outdoor Spaces for People with Dementia*. Australia: Hammond Press.

Stoneham, Jane and Peter Thoday.1994. *Landscape Design for Elderly and Disabled People*. UK: Packard Publishing Ltd.

Wagenfeld, Amy and Winterbottom, Daniel. 2015. *Therapeutic Gardens: Design for Healing Spaces*. Portland, OR: Timber Press.

Cooper Marcus, Clare and Marni Barnes, eds.1999. *Healing Gardens, Therapeutic Benefits and Design Recommendations*. New York: John Wiley and Sons, Inc.

NURTURING NATURE

INFORMATION AND ADAPTIVE SUPPLIES FOR SPECIAL POPULATIONS

"Gardening When Blind Or Visually Impaired," Thrive: Using Gardening to Change Lives, accessed January 5, 2024, https://www.thrive.org.uk/get-gardening/gardening-when-blind-or-visually-impaired#.

Adaptive Tools and Equipment*

"Health Care Products That Make Life Easier/ Adaptive Daily Living Aids," The Wright Stuff: accessed January 28, 2024, https://www.thewrightstuff.com/Garden-Tools_c_192-2-4.html.

Toni DeBella. "8 Best Garden Scooters for Easy Gardening," *Family Handyman*, 11/13/2023. https://www.familyhandyman.com/list/best-garden-scooters/.

Supplies for Special Activities*

Butterfly Grow Kits: Nature Gift Store, accessed January 27, 2024, https://www.nature-gifts.com/shop/grow-butterflies/.

Insect Lore, accessed January 27, 2024, https://www.insectlore.com/collections/butterflies-butterfly-kits-with-live-caterpillars.

Worm Farm Kits and Supplies, accessed January 27, 2024, https://unclejimswormfarm.com/.

BOOKS THAT HAVE INSPIRED ME

Florence Williams. 2017. T*he Nature Fix: Why Nature Makes Us Happier, Healthier, and More Creative*. New York: W. W. Norton Company.

Barbara Kingsolver, Camille Kingsolver, Steven L. Hopp, Lily Hopp Kingsolver. 2017. *Animal, Vegetable, Miracle: A Year of Food Life*. New York: Harper Perennial.

Novella Carpenter. 2010. Farm City: *The Education of an Urban Farmer*. London: Penguin Books.

Kristin Kimball. 2010. *The Dirty Life: A Memoir of Farming, Food, and Love*. New York: Scribner.

Peter Wohllben. 2015. *The Hidden Life of Trees What They Feel, How They Communicate*. Canada: Greystone Books.

Michael Pollan. 2007. *The Omnivore's Dilemma: A Natural History of Four Meals*. London: Penguin.

Robin Wall Kimmerer. 2013. *Braiding Sweetgrass Indigenous Wisdom, Scientific Knowledge, and the Teaching of Plants*. Canada: Milkweed Editions.

* These are examples and not officially endorsed by the author.

Resources

BOOKS THAT HAVE EDUCATED ME IN THE WAYS OF GARDENING

Eliot Coleman. 2009. *The Winter Harvest Handbook Year-Round Vegetable Production Using Deep-Organic Techniques and Unheated Greenhouses*. White River Junction, Vermont: Chelsea Green Publishing.

Allison Greer. 2019. *Companion Planting: Organic Gardening Tips and Tricks for Healthier, Happier Plants*. New York: Skyhorse Publishing.

Margaret Roach. *A Way to Garden Online*, accessed, January 27, 2024.

BOOKS FOR GARDENING WITH CHILDREN

M. Hannemann, P. Hulse, B. Johnson, B. Kurland, T. Patterson, Illustrator: Sm Tomasello, Editor: S. Wolff Saphire. 2015. *Gardening with Children*. New York: Brooklyn Botanical Garden – All Regions Guides.

Kirsten Bradley, Illustrator: Aitch, Editors: Angela Francis and Robert Klanten. 2019. *Easy Peasy Gardening for Kids*. New York: Little Gestalten.

Renata Fossen Brown. 2014. *Gardening Lab for Kids: 52 Fun Experiments to Learn, Grow, Harvest, Make, Play, and Enjoy Your Garden*. London: Quarry Books.

George Ancona. 2015. *It's Our Garden – From Seeds to Harvest in a School Garden*. Somerville, Massachusetts: Candlewick Press.

John Allan. 2019. *Amazing Life Cycles – Plants*. Truro, England: Hungry Tomato.

STEM SERIES

Richard Lay, Illustrator: Laura Zarrin, Editors: S. Hedlund, R. Baltzer. 2013. *A Green Kids Guide to: Gardening!* New York: Looking Glass Library.

Rebecca Pettiford. 2015. *Way to Grow! Gardening: Vegetables*. Minneapolis, Minnesota: Jump!

Kay Barnham, Maddie Frost. 2018. *The Amazing Life Cycle of Butterflies*. Naperville, Illinois: Sourcebooks.

Kay Barnham, Maddie Frost. 2018. *The Amazing Life Cycle of Plants*. Naperville, Illinois: Sourcebooks.

ACKNOWLEDGMENTS

Francie Randolph welcomed me to the Truro's Children's Garden and introduced me to a community of farmers and the Sustainable CAPE organization. By including me in their mission: to celebrate local food while educating about the health of our bodies, community, and environment, I have been inspired to write this book. Stephanie Rein—educator extraordinaire, developed a program in conjunction with Sustainable CAPE to engage children in farming at school. Many of the activities listed in this book come from her *Farmer in the School* curriculum. I have also gleaned much from the lead farmers for the Truro Children's Garden program: Anna, Jess Drake, Cynthia and Sarah.

The Truro Library has been instrumental in all aspects of my community engagement with gardening and more. A very special thanks to Maggie Hanelt, the Assistant Director and Director of Youth Services, for facilitating my involvement with the Children's Garden program and Cape Abilities. In addition, Maggie has read several of my unpublished manuscripts and assisted in research. I also wish to pay tribute to the Payomet people of the Wampanoag Nation. The Truro Children's Community Garden is sited on unceded land of the Wampanoag Nation, and I want to thank them for their stewardship of this land in the past, present and future.

I have thoroughly enjoyed collaborating with Cape Abilities, which supports individuals with disabilities on Cape Cod, by educating, counseling and providing residential, therapeutic social and employment supports that empower individuals to achieve meaningful roles in the community. Thank you for your vision in seeing the benefits of gardening in Truro and at the Cape Abilities Farm.

NURTURING NATURE

I owe a huge thanks to Florence Williams. *The Nature Fix* was the spark that led to this book. I've been a proponent of sensory motor and nature-based play throughout my career. When I read Williams' exceptional treatise enumerating the scientific evidence of nature's critical role in keeping us healthy and happy, I knew this had to be shared with the populations I serve. Thank you to Jennifer Gilpin Yacio for believing in this book along with the Future Horizons team, especially Karen South, John Yacio, and Susan Thompson for your help.

Thank you to my readers: Rachael Barabel, Meribeth Howlett, Annmarie Chang, and John Snow for providing valuable feedback. Thanks to Christene Tashjian for sharing your expertise in aroma and horticulture therapies. I also want to thank those who have read multiple manuscripts that I have written. While these stories have yet to be published, you have encouraged and inspired me to stay the course and keep writing: Shari Stahl, Deb Besemer, Claire Aniello, Diane Antezzo, Kathy Sharpless and the Truro Library writing group.

Thank you Christopher and Bobby for allowing me to share your images in both of my Future Horizons books. Thanks Ben for the tutorial on Google Docs. Thank you Kate! It takes courage for a daughter to critique a mother's work. Your brilliant feedback and editorial insights have polished my writing in all five of my major writing projects!

Eric, while painstakingly doing line edits, you must have noticed I wrote *MY GARDEN* throughout the narrative, but it truly is *OUR GARDEN*. I'm so glad that we embarked on this garden journey together, and eternally grateful for all your heavy lifting, in the garden, and in all aspects of our lives.

ABOUT THE AUTHOR

Photo by Fancie Randolph

Jill Mays is the author of *Your Child's Motor Development Story,* highlighting the critical importance of sensory exploration and natural play for healthy development. An occupational therapist specializing in sensory integration for many years, she has conducted workshops in a variety of settings and provided consultation to parents, educators and health care providers. For the past ten years she has immersed herself in gardening, working with farmers and assisting in the development of children's garden programs. She developed and currently leads a garden group for special needs adults. Jill lives with her husband, Eric, their Portuguese Water Dog and a flock of chickens at the far end of Cape Cod.

Also by the author

**YOUR CHILD'S
MOTOR
DEVELOPMENT
ST🖐RY**

Understanding and Enhancing Development
from Birth to Their First Sport

Jill Howlett Mays, MS, OTR/L

  (817) 277-0727 | www.fhautism.com

Printed in the USA
CPSIA information can be obtained
at www.ICGtesting.com
JSHW011823260924
70554JS00003B/4

9 781963 367058